# SPEAK, LORD, YOUR SERVANT IS LISTENING

# SPEAK, LORD
# Your Servant Is
# Listening

Msgr. David E. Rosage

Servant Books
Ann Arbor, Michigan

Copyright © 1987 Msgr. David E. Rosage
All rights reserved.

Cover design by Michael P. Andaloro
Cover photograph by Howard M. DeCruyenaere

Servant Books
Box 8617
Ann Arbor, Michigan 48107

ISBN 0-89283-371-8
Printed in the United States of America

99  12  11  10

# Contents

# Foreword

The first edition of *Speak, Lord, Your Servant Is Listening* has been appreciatively received. Many have found the prayer tips along with the suggested scriptural passages for each day a helpful guide for entering more deeply into prayer of the heart.

As a handbook, it has become a popular daily companion. It has been described by a carpenter as a "lunch bucket book," by a missionary in Africa as a "good motorcar book," by a business woman as a "handy purse-size companion."

In this new edition, new chapters have been added describing how one can assume a more relaxed, contemplative posture as one prays. These thoughts should facilitate making the transition from the busy workaday world into a quiet, receptive attitude of listening to God with one's whole being. They should also motivate one to become totally available to the Lord.

This handbook is offered with the prayer that all who use it may generously say, "Speak, LORD, for your servant is listening" (1 Samuel 3:9).

— David E. Rosage

# Introduction

The title, *Speak, Lord, Your Servant Is Listening,* suggests the reason for this volume. It is presented with the hope of meeting a crucial need. God has placed in many hearts a longing for a more personal experience of him in prayer, a desire for a more intimate relationship with him. St. Paul is eager to advise us that this very hunger is from God himself. "It is God who, in his good will toward you, begets in you any measure of desire or achievement" (Philippians 2:13).

Seeking a deeper relationship with God, many have been led to sacred Scripture as a basis for prayer. As we approach the Word of God with a listening heart, we become more and more aware of the Lord's loving, abiding presence with us. *Speak, Lord, Your Servant Is Listening* is a response to an oft-repeated request for some kind of outline or guide to lead one through God's Word more profitably.

This book suggests a passage of Scripture for each day of the fifty-two weeks of the year. The theme for each week is arranged to correspond roughly to the order of the meditations and contemplations of a thirty-day retreat according to the *Spiritual Exercises* of St. Ignatius of Loyola. A similar outline can also be used for what is sometimes called the 19th Annotation retreat. If the first week of the outline is begun in September, the themes will coincide with the annual liturgical cycle.

The procedure for using this manual is very simple. First, find a regular time for daily prayer. Fifteen or twenty minutes will probably be enough at first, although you may find yourself drawn to spend more time with the Lord as your relationship with him deepens. Second, find a suitable place where you can be still and listen to the Lord in quiet. You may choose a chapel, bedroom, den, or any place where you are relaxed and comfortable.

Once you are settled, turn to the passage of Scripture suggested for that day according to the week and day you have reached in the outline. Read the passage slowly and reflectively. It may be helpful to read it aloud. Let the words sink in. Let them find a home in your heart.

9

Use your imagination to picture the action or scene described, then try to enter into it. Try to experience what is happening or listen to what is being said. As you try to listen to what the Lord is saying to you through his Word, you may be moved to respond with gratitude, praise, or an expression of love — whatever seems appropriate.

On the left-hand side of the pages of this book you will find some suggestions for prayer for each week of the year. These suggestions are not necessarily connected with the weekly theme. Instead, they will help you gain a deeper understanding of prayer.

May you have a happy, peaceful, prayerful journey with the Lord!

# Part One

ONE

# The Age of the Holy Spirit

Our age has been characterized as the age of the Holy Spirit. History will only serve to authenticate this claim. We have ample evidence of the Holy Spirit persistently calling us as individuals and as the church to a deeper awakening. The power of the Holy Spirit is evident in movements all over the world, movements through which God is inviting Christians to be more committed to him.

What is taking place in the world today is reminiscent of the dynamism and power of the Holy Spirit in the early church. On various occasions, the Holy Spirit manifested his presence and power as the apostles proclaimed the good news. Some of the unusual manifestations of the Holy Spirit's presence took place in Samaria (Acts 8:14), Caesarea (Acts 10:44), Ephesus (Acts 19:1). These happenings are sometimes considered minor Pentecosts.

When Pope John XXIII convoked the Second Vatican Council, he invited the whole world to pray with him: ''O Holy Spirit . . . pour forth the fullness of your gifts. . . . Renew your wonders in this our day as by a new Pentecost.'' This prayer daily continues to be answered. The church is, in fact, experiencing a new Pentecost.

The Holy Spirit's inspiration and power is apparent in many different movements today. For example, the Cursillo emphasizes conversion and community. It has changed many people's lives and turned them toward God. Similarly, the charismatic renewal has set thousands on a journey toward more dedicated Christian service. It has spawned a vital awareness of the presence of the Spirit promised by Jesus.

13

Various programs have been established to renew family life and strengthen this fundamental unit of society. Gatherings such as "Marriage Encounter" and couples' retreats, to mention only two, have inspired men and women to dedicate themselves to healthy marriages and family life.

The growing popularity of directed retreats is indicative of the Spirit drawing us into deeper communion with God. At the heart of these retreats is scriptural prayer.

The increasing number of Christian communities is also a response to the Holy Spirit's work of drawing more people into spiritual renewal. These communities meet an important need especially in third world countries.

How has the Holy Spirit accomplished such great works in the lives of so many? Allow me to examine the various levels on which the Holy Spirit operates in men and women. This examination will enable us to see the depth of his transforming power. In turn, we will learn how to yield more fully to divine influence.

## Level One

The Holy Spirit touches each one of us in various ways and on different levels. Every one of us has some experience of the presence of the Holy Spirit within us, perhaps without even being aware of it.

We are naturally drawn to what is good and beautiful. We are attracted to the innocent. We want justice to prevail. Above all, we want to love and be loved. All these inclinations are due to the power of the Spirit of Jesus dwelling within us. We have an innate emotional response to what is good.

Most of our time is spent living on this level of feeling. However, feelings do not always lead us to righteousness. Our instincts can often conflict with proper values. Often we base our judgments on what feels good, believing that if something feels good it then must be right. Or it must be right because everyone else is doing it. If it is a fashion, then it must be good.

Living only on this level of feeling brings great turmoil. In order for the Holy Spirit to work more deeply within us, our seed of faith must germinate and be nurtured.

## Level Two

The Spirit also exerts influence on our intellects. As we mature and become more open to the Holy Spirit, he touches our minds so we can begin to comprehend God's truth. While it is more conducive to our well-being to live on this level than on the first, reason will not satisfy us completely.

If we rely solely on our intellect, we will experience many difficulties. With our intellect we can make some good judgments, but reason alone cannot conquer vacillating, unreliable emotions nor can it lead us to a deeper knowledge of God and his ways.

## Level Three

The Spirit of Jesus can move us beyond our emotions and reason to the very center of ourselves where the Spirit dwells and where spiritual maturity develops. God works most profoundly in our hearts.

Solitude with the Lord and a sincere desire to know God and ourselves are indispensable conditions for hearing the voice of the Lord. Here we are not dependent on sensation and emotion. We move beyond an intellectual or theological knowledge of God, beyond head knowledge to heart knowledge. It is in the center of our beings, in our hearts, where we fully recognize God as a personal God. This level of knowing God is the gift of the Holy Spirit.

When we listen to God's Word and receive it into our hearts, the Holy Spirit speaks to us with great clarity. St. Paul describes the fruit of this kind of prayerful listening:

> All Scripture is inspired of God and is useful for teaching — for reproof, correction, and training in holiness so that the man of God may be fully competent and equipped for every good work. (2 Timothy 3:16)

God personally speaks to us through his Word. When we listen to Scripture with sincere, receptive hearts, we receive inspiration which we may have never discovered before. We gain a broader vision of the divine.

Scripture is not an end in itself but a means of bringing us closer to the Lord. When we pray in this way, our spirits are open to the message the Holy Spirit wishes to convey to us personally and individually. We are made more fully aware of the magnitude of God's love for us regardless of who we are or what we have done. We can discern and understand what God expects of us and see more clearly what he wishes for us today, tomorrow, and all the days which lie ahead.

Scriptural prayer bears much fruit. The following is a list of what we can expect when we pray:

1. We will discover that we are not alone. God begins to communicate with us. We are reminded of the Lord's promise: ''Know that I am with you always, until the end of the world'' (Matthew 28:20).

2. At first we will discover no discernible insights nor any intellectual challenges; however, we will experience peace, joy, and well-being.

3. If we faithfully meet with the Lord, we will begin to know ourselves a little better. We will notice that all the past — including our failures — fit into a definite pattern. God's plan for our lives becomes clearer. Life has more meaning.

4. Next we will experience a spontaneous sense of gratitude for all we have received. We may not necessarily think of specific objects of gratitude, but we will be able to see his provision and faithfulness throughout our lives. Without realizing it, our gratitude toward God will intensify. Only a grateful person becomes a prayerful person.

Consequently, our gratitude will allow us to love others freely. Acknowledging God's love and abiding presence in our lives empowers us to love others more deeply and selflessly.

We will discover that the Lord wants us to be happy and to succeed in all that we do. Gradually, as we turn our lives over to him, we will find greater happiness and success.

The first time we pray with Scripture we may not experience a profound richness in the words or gain great insight into their meaning; however, we will experience a sense of peace and joy. If we share our experience with another person, these fruits will be magnified within us.

We will find fresh meaning even in passages we may have

read many times before. We will also find that the words we read will come back to us during the course of the day. In short, Scripture will become the backbone of our daily lives and will shape our spiritual growth and maturation.

## Procedure

Bible passages should be read slowly so that every word sinks in and finds a home in our hearts. In this way the meaning of a word, a phrase, or a verse will be grasped and understood with our hearts rather than merely with our heads.

This type of reflective reading can be compared to gazing intently at a work of art, sipping a delicate wine, or listening to music. God's Word must be read slowly and savored. There is no need to analyze the words or "work" the text. Just listen quietly with the attitude: "Lord, what are you saying to me today through these words?"

Some days we may simply want to bask in his love, thus coming to a greater conviction that we are loved and lovable. As we wait and relax in his presence, we may feel deep gratitude for all the Lord has done for us.

Praying with Scripture should never become a Bible study. Nor should we try to find the objective meaning of the text. It is true that the more we know about the Bible the better our prayer will be, but studying the Bible should not be confused with praying the Word of God.

What the Lord may want to say to us in the passage may not be the meaning of the text. This should not disturb us, since the words of the Scripture are the means whereby we can encounter God. It is like an elevator lifting us above the mundane and bringing us into God's presence.

A lamp to my feet is your word,
    a light to my path. (Psalm 119:105)
Blest are they who hear the word of God and keep it.
(Luke 11:28)

## Our Source of Unity

The presence and power of the Holy Spirit operates in the sacramental life of the church, especially in the Sacraments of Baptism and Confirmation.

In Baptism we are adopted by the Father, engrafted into Christ, and made temples of the Holy Spirit. St. Paul's words leave no room for doubt:

> You must know that your body is a temple of the Holy Spirit, who is within — the Spirit you have received from God. You are not your own. You have been purchased, and at a price! So glorify God in your body. (1 Corinthians 6:19-20)

The Holy Spirit is the very essence of divine love which is the matrix uniting Christians in mind and heart. Community cannot be built solely on rules and regulations. It must be built on love. In Baptism we have received the divine life and love of the Holy Spirit in an extraordinary way. "The love of God has been poured out in our hearts through the Holy Spirit who has been given to us" (Romans 5:5).

The Spirit within us is a dynamic presence. If we are receptive and cooperative, he will endow us with the fruit of the Spirit: "Love, joy, peace, patient endurance, kindness, generosity, faith, mildness and chastity" (Galations 5:22).

## The Builder of Community

The Holy Spirit establishes unity among Christians. In Ephesians 4:1-16, St. Paul speaks eloquently about the unity which must be preserved in the mystical body of Christ. In verse 3, he admonishes us: "Make every effort to preserve the unity which has the Spirit as its origin and peace as its binding force."

In Baptism we are incorporated into the body of Christ. This incorporation establishes a unique and mysterious relationship. Our loving Father adopts us as his sons and daughters. "I will welcome you and be a father to you and you will be my sons and daughters" (2 Corinthians 6:18). In Romans we are reminded that all who are led by the Spirit are the sons and daughters of God which enables us to call God "Abba, Father" (Romans 8:15).

Our adoption constitutes a very special relationship with our kind and compassionate Father. It helps us recognize the great privilege and dignity which are ours as a person, as a Christian, as members of his kingdom.

Since we have a common Father, we are in a very real sense

brothers and sisters. If we love God and our brothers and sisters as well as ourselves, then we are laying a firm foundation for Christian community.

Baptism destines us for community. We are baptized into the Trinitarian community, a community of perfect love between the Father, Son, and Holy Spirit. God created within each of us a capacity to enjoy heavenly communion even while we sojourn on this earth.

## Confirmation

Confirmation is a sacrament of maturity. When we receive this sacrament, we are further empowered to fulfill our special ministry in the community. We are endowed with special gifts of the Spirit which enable us to fulfill our function in the body of Christ. The gifts of the Holy Spirit are not given solely for our own spiritual growth but for our specific role of service in the community. Paul explains this truth:

Just as each of us has one body with many members, and not all the members have the same function, so too we, though many, are one body in Christ and individually members one of another. We have gifts that differ according to the favor bestowed on each of us. (Romans 12:4)

The Holy Spirit builds community. In order for the Spirit to work, we must establish the proper conditions. We must exhibit loving concern for one another. The members of a community must be willing to share with one another. They must share their joys and sorrows, their time, talents, and sometimes their treasures. Above all, they must share their prayer. There is no more powerful force in establishing community than praying together.

Love is the foundation of all interpersonal relationships. We cannot love others we do not know, and we cannot know them unless we share ourselves with them and they with us. Praying with one another is a way of sharing ourselves more intimately.

In order for the Holy Spirit to mold and transform us, we must spend time regularly listening to God in solitude and stillness — in prayer of the heart. Just as an individual, praying con-

19

templatively with Scripture, experiences the Holy Spirit's consolations, directions, and exhortations for his spiritual growth, likewise, the community, listening and praying with God's Word, finds together God's will and directions for them as a body. The community as a whole experiences God's love and expresses his favor as its members reach out in loving concern to those outside the community.

All this is the work of the Holy Spirit; therefore, we pray fervently: "Come, Holy Spirit."

# TWO

# From Cosmic to Celestial Communication

Good communication is essential to establishing and maintaining comfortable relationships. Honest and open communication reveals our appreciation and affection for those dear to us. It also enriches our own personal life as well as the lives of family and friends.

However, a lack of communication or poor communication can fracture what might otherwise be a happy, wholesome relationship. An absence of communication can create misunderstandings, confusion, and tension.

Socially, sincere communication expresses our interest and concern for others. This adds to our enjoyment of life and blesses all those with whom we associate.

In the business world, efficient communication is essential. Clear, precise, intelligent communication keeps business operations running profitably. It is the key to success or failure in some business ventures. Good communication between the administration and other personnel not only creates pleasant working conditions but also greatly contributes to the success of any organization.

## Avenues of Communicating

We can communicate in a variety of ways. Our personal presence and our face-to-face conversation speak eloquently to another person. Our words and posture can express affection and concern or reveal our indifference and even antagonism.

If we cannot be present with a person, we can communicate

by telephone or write a letter. Hearing a voice over the telephone gives us a sense of presence. A letter also makes the sender present to us. We can almost hear the sound of the person's voice or recognize their thought pattern. A letter also tells us that the sender cares enough to write.

Our modern technology has created a fabulous system of instant communication. Radio, television, conference telephones, and computers spread their messages far and wide. Communications via satellite bring us instant news, keeping us informed of what is happening around the world. Modern technology allows us to hear and see astronauts on the moon. These sophisticated systems of communication are spectacular and fabulous. Our inventions prove the tremendous importance that human beings place on communication.

## Beyond Technology

As astounding as our achievements in communications may be, they are dwarfed by another far superior and more magnificent means of communication which requires neither batteries nor transistors. You and I can penetrate time and space; we can go beyond all the miracles of technology. We can enter the realm of the supernatural by communicating with the transcendent God, the Creator of heaven and earth. Incredible as it may seem, we can be in direct contact with the Creator and Sustainer of the entire universe. The only requirement is a listening, receptive heart.

What is even more incredible is that God wants to communicate with each one of us personally. In fact, the Lord and Master of the universe waits for us to come to him and hear his voice. He wants to communicate with us even more than we desire it ourselves. That is the mystery of his love for us.

## Divine Communication

God communicates with us in a myriad of ways. Our physical senses can easily bring us into an awareness of the beauty and intricacy of God's creative genius. The song of the bird, the touch of a loved one, the fragrance of a flower are all channels which God uses to reveal himself to us. Our physical senses can keep us in constant contact with our loving Father.

Our inner senses are also pathways which lead us to God. Through these senses we experience the peace and joy which only God can give. Nothing can compare with the inner knowledge that we are loved by our compassionate God.

Our minds — our capacity to reason and comprehend — should engender awe, reverence, and wonder within us. God has made us thinking, creative beings after his own image and likeness. And he has given us hearts capable of receiving his love. He knows our source of happiness, peace, and joy comes only from his profound love for us.

Hearing from God does not require any technical know-how or any modern, sophisticated equipment. All that is necessary is a quiet, receptive heart. We need to give God time, to come before him unprotected, to listen to him with our whole being.

This prompted the psalmist's admonitions, "Be still and know that I am God" (Psalm 46:10). "Leave it to the LORD, / and wait for him" (Psalm 37:7). "Wait for the LORD, / and keep his way" (Psalm 37:34).

## God's Word

Some people maintain that God speaks to us through the signs of the times such as earthquakes, floods, tornadoes, and other natural disasters. Others carry it one step further. They insist that as man rebels against God, nature in turn rebels against man. Directly or indirectly there may be some truth in these assertions since these tragic, destructive phenomena do remind us of our limitations and the might and power of the Lord.

In our prayer, however, God communicates in a gentle, peaceful, quiet way. Thus he spoke to Elijah when he sought asylum on Mount Horeb. Here Elijah found that God was not present in the strong and mighty wind or in the earthquake or in fire, but Elijah heard his voice in a "tiny whispering sound" (1 Kings 19:12). Such is the gentleness of God's voice when we come to meet him in the stillness and solitude of prayer.

God uses sacred Scripture to speak his mind and heart to us. The Bible is not simply an account of salvation history. It is not merely a collection of theological reflections on God's actions in human history. Indeed, God's Word is as living and effective today as it was the day it was spoken. It is by no means out-of-date or obsolete. Jesus himself promised that the Holy Spirit would "instruct you in everything, and remind you of all that I told you" (John 14:26); furthermore, "when he comes, however, being the Spirit of truth he will guide you to all truth" (John 16:13).

The Second Vatican Council reminds us that "He (Jesus) is present in His word, since it is He who speaks when the Holy Scriptures are read in the Church" (Const. Lit. par. 7). Jesus speaks his Word to us to inspire, motivate, encourage, comfort, and fulfill us.

## Two Avenues

We can approach the Scriptures with two different intentions. We may wish to know more about the Word of God by spending time studying the Bible. This is highly commendable, since the better we know the Bible the deeper and richer our prayers will be. However, this intellectual or exegetical approach, while extremely beneficial, is not yet prayer.

Praying with Scripture consists primarily of listening to what the Lord is saying to us in his Word. Listening does not mean straining and striving to hear words spoken by the Lord. It means being open and receptive to the inspiration, awareness, or experience of God which may come to us. Being available to the Lord will permit his Word to find a home in our heart. His Word has the power to produce many wonderful fruits in us. Just as the Father sends forth the rain and the snow to water the earth, so too he sends his Word into our hearts with the assurance: "It shall not return to me void, but shall do my will, achieving the end for which I sent it" (Isaiah 55:11).

Many people are searching for some kind of fulfillment in their daily existence. Without being aware of it, they are searching for an experience of God in their lives. They long for some experiential awareness of his presence and love. Some do not recognize this longing for God and seek fulfillment in various escape routes. They become restless, disillusioned, and frustrated. Unfortunately, they turn to some disastrous escapes such as an insatiable desire for pleasure, a consuming involvement in busyness, or even a dependence on chemical substances.

However, there are countless people who in the process of searching for God have discovered a new and exciting dimension to their prayer life by using Scripture as a basis for their prayer. This obviously is the influence of the Holy Spirit in these important days of spiritual reawakening. The very desire is a gift of the Spirit as St. Paul informs us: "It is God who, in his good will toward you, begets in you any measure of desire or achievement" (Philippians 2:13).

The inspired Word of God is the work of the Trinity. All three Persons invite us to listen with our whole being to the divine words found in Scripture. They urge us to permit these words to dwell within us so that their power and fruit may be released in our lives.

## The Father's Request

"Come to me heedfully, listen, that you may have life" (Isaiah 55:3). The Father assures us that his Word will not only lead us to eternal life but will guarantee us a vibrant spiritual health and also physical well-being.

On Mount Tabor the Father's request became more direct and imperative. Jesus had completed his teaching mission of proclaiming the good news. Now he was about to enter his redemptive work by laying down his life for us and rising again from the dead. The Father confirms Jesus' mission with these words: "This is my beloved Son on whom my favor rests," and then follows his paternal directive — brief, but to the point: "Listen to him" (Matthew 17:5).

## Jesus Invites Us

On many occasions Jesus pleaded with his followers to listen intently to him. He asked them and us to listen with our whole being so that his words may become a way of life for us. "Rather, blest are they who hear the word of God and keep it" (Luke 11:28).

As we join the crowd on the lakeshore and listen to Jesus narrate the parable of the sower sowing his seed, we cannot help but be convicted by his words. How simply yet profoundly Jesus illustrates the necessity of receiving and nurturing his words,

25

the seeds of life. Then Jesus makes his point: ''Let him who has ears to hear me, hear! . . . Listen carefully to what you hear'' (Mark 4:23-24).

We are well aware of the popular image of Jesus as the good shepherd. Here again Jesus emphasizes the importance of listening. Speaking of himself as the good shepherd, he says: ''The sheep hear his voice as he calls his own by name and leads them out. . . . the sheep follow him because they recognize his voice'' (John 10:3-4).

## The Holy Spirit Urges Us

''The Spirit too helps us in our weakness, for we do not know how to pray as we ought; but the Spirit himself makes intercession for us . . . (Romans 8:26). The Spirit is at work on our behalf as we pray with a listening heart. He not only intercedes for us but empowers us, dwells more fully inside of us, and even transforms our being as we yield to him.

In the Book of Revelation the Spirit speaks to us about listening: ''Happy is the man who reads this prophetic message, and happy are those who hear it and heed what is written in it'' (Revelations 1:3). ''Let him who has ears heed the Spirit's word'' (Revelations 2:7, 11, 17, 29; 3:13, 22).

Today more than ever, we are being called by God to a prayer posture of listening at the very core of our being.

*Part Two*

# WEEK 1

## Prayer Is Hunger

God is putting in our hearts a genuine hunger for a more intimate personal relationship with him, a relationship nurtured through a life of prayer. He invites us to listen to what he says to us through his Word in Scripture. As we listen, we become more aware of his loving presence within us.

This awareness and our response is a contemplative prayer posture. As we pray with Scripture, a transformation takes place within us. Our personal relationship with the Lord develops, and we acquire a fresh, spiritual way of thinking. We develop a new mentality as our minds become conformed to the mind of Christ.

As we listen, God reveals more and more about himself. We learn that he is a God who knows everything about us. We discover that he loves us with a creative, providential, forgiving, healing, redeeming love.

We must approach our praying with Scripture with this attitude: "What is God saying to me here and now?" The Fathers of the Vatican Council assured us that "(Christ) is present in his Word, since it is he himself who speaks when the holy Scriptures are read in the Church." If Christ is present, then he is speaking to us. We in turn must listen quietly in our hearts.

# God's Invitation

The theme for this week's prayer is a consideration of God's special invitation to you personally. He is inviting you to come to him that he may bestow his gifts upon you, particularly the gift of his divine life—the gift of himself. He tells us that his gifts come at no cost other than our willingness to accept and use them. St. Paul tells us that even our eternal salvation is a gift from God.

In the suggested readings for this week, you will notice that one scriptural passage is listed for each day. These texts carry out the theme of God inviting you.

**First Day—Isaiah 55:1-13**
An invitation to grace: "Come to the water! . . . come, receive grain and eat."

**Second Day—Jeremiah 1:4-10**
God calls us as he did the prophet: "Before I formed you in the womb I knew you."

**Third Day—Psalm 95**
The psalmist invites us to praise God for calling us to know him.

**Fourth Day—Mark 6:30-44**
Jesus invites us to come apart and rest awhile.

**Fifth Day—Matthew 11:28-30**
Jesus invites us to come to him when we are beset with problems and anxieties.

**Sixth Day—Revelation 3:14-22**
Jesus invites us to repentance: "Here I stand, knocking at the door."

**Seventh Day—John 14:1-15**
"I am indeed going to prepare a place for you, and then I shall come back to take you with me."

## Listening

Prayer is a communication with God, and communication is a two-way street. To have a good communication we must speak, but we must also listen. That's the rub. We hear a great deal each day, but we listen very seldom. Listening is an art and must be practiced.

Furthermore, in communicating, the person who has the most important message should have more time. Now, in prayer it is quite obvious who has the most important message; therefore, we should spend much more time in listening to God than in speaking to him. I think one of the common difficulties in prayer is that we do most of the speaking and very little listening.

Since prayer is a communication between God and ourselves, and since what God has to say is far more important than what we have to talk over with him, then the first requisite for prayer is that we learn to listen.

In our eagerness to enter quickly and deeply into prayer, we often begin by thanking God for some favor, or apprising him of some situation, or simply asking him to come and help us do our thing. We feel that to just sit or kneel and do nothing is a waste of time. Waiting and listening seem to be so impractical. That's why the psalmist reminds us: ''Be still before the Lord and wait patiently on him'' (Psalm 37:7 RSV).

As long as the focus is on ourselves, we will have difficulties in praying. Our focus must be on God. God wants to speak to us. He wants us to listen in the quiet of our own being, and only then respond in our hearts.

# Listen to God Speaking to You Through His Word

It is not only startling, but even mysterious, to consider that the transcendent God of heaven and earth wishes to communicate with me, a tiny grain of sand in this immense universe. Unbelievable as it may seem, it is true. God does want to speak to us, especially through his Word. He does not shout, nor does he force us to pause in our hurry-filled life, but he does invite us to "Come aside and rest awhile." He does say of us: "I will lead her into the desert and speak to her heart" (Hosea 2:16).

This week let us listen to what he has to say to us in the Old Testament.

**First Day—Isaiah 55:1-3, 10, 11**
"My word. . . . shall not return to me void."

**Second Day—Jeremiah 7:1-15**
"You did not answer, though I called." "You did not listen, though I spoke to you untiringly."

**Third Day—Jeremiah 23:16-29**
"Is not my word like fire . . . like a hammer shattering rocks?"

**Fourth Day—Hosea 6:1-6**
The Word of God wants love, not empty sacrifice.

**Fifth Day—Wisdom 18:14-16**
"Your all-powerful word from heaven's royal throne."

**Sixth Day—Psalm 8**
The majesty of God and the dignity of man: "O Lord, our Lord, how glorious is your name over all the earth!"

**Seventh Day—Psalm 19**
"The heavens declare the glory of God." (In this psalm, "law," "decree," "precepts," "command" are synonyms of "word.")

# WEEK 3

## Hearken

The word we find most frequently used in Scripture is the name of God with his many titles. Running a close second is the word "Listen" and its numerous synonyms: hearken, attend, pay attention, open your ears, hear, and others. This fact is significant because it tells us how important it is for us to listen to God's Word as handed down in the Bible. God's Word is creative, powerful, encouraging, instructive, cleansing and comforting.

The psalmist does not want us to take the Word of God lightly. He pleads, "Oh, that today you would hear his voice, 'Harden not your hearts' " (Psalm 95:7-8).

In recent years there has been a new upsurge of interest in God's Word. The many new and popular translations of the Bible have made the reading and praying of God's Word easy and enjoyable. There are numerous courses and study groups offered to help us understand the Bible a little better. All these are important and very necessary.

Most important, however, the Bible is rapidly becoming a "prayerbook" for more and more people. It is so essential to read and reflect on God's Word as handed down to us in the pages of Scripture. Without the Bible, there can be no authentic Christianity. There can be no genuine religious formation which is not based and rooted in the gospel message. The Bible is God's personal message to you and to me. What would you think of a person who received a letter from a very dear friend and never bothered to open it? Does not God's Word receive the same treatment from us many times?

The scriptural readings suggested above and the theme we offer here is an attempt to help us use God's Word as the source and basis of our prayer.

# God Is Speaking to Me

It is not easy for us to comprehend the momentous truth that the transcendent God of heaven and earth, the Creator of the entire universe, wishes to communicate with us personally. Yet it is true. God is a universal God, but he is also an exclusive God. That is why he wants to speak to us personally. God wants to communicate with each one of us through his Word, not only through the words on the printed page, but also through his voiceless voice within us. He speaks to us, as it were, between the lines. The following New Testament scriptural references for our praying demonstrate the import of his word in our lives:

**First Day—Romans 10:8-17**
"The word is near you, on your lips and in your heart. . . . Faith then, comes through hearing, and what is heard is the word of Christ."

**Second Day—2 Timothy 3:14-17**
"All Scripture is inspired by God and is useful for teaching."

**Third Day—Matthew 13:1-23**
"Blest are your ears because they hear."

**Fourth Day—John 1:1-14**
"The Word became flesh . . ."

**Fifth Day—1 John 1:1-10**
"We speak of the word of life."

**Sixth Day—2 Thessalonians 2:13-17**
You have been chosen: "He called you by our preaching . . . . may God . . . strengthen [you] for every good work and word."

**Seventh Day—1 Thessalonians 1:2-6; 2:13**
"You took it, not as the word of men, but as it truly is, the word of God."

# God Speaks

It is impossible for us to know a person very well until we have heard him speak. The more he talks, the better we get to know him. By his speech he reveals very much about himself — his hopes and ambitions, his joys and sorrows, his likes and dislikes, his whole philosophy of life. In short, he tells us what kind of a person he is. If we listen intently, we will discover very much about him.

This is also true of God. We can best know God as he reveals himself to us through his Word. St. Jerome puts it very bluntly: "Ignorance of the Scripture is ignorance of Christ." Yes, God does reveal much about his nature as we listen to his Word. It is also true that the more intently we listen to God, the better we will come to know him.

What does God tell us about himself? He reveals that he is a God of power and might: God spoke and the universe came into being. He tells us that he is a God who is concerned about us every moment of the day. Yes, he knows when we stand and when we sit. He knows every thought before it comes into our mind and every word before it is on our lips (Psalm 139).

He not only tells us, but he proves to us that he is a God who really loves us: "With age-old love I have loved you" (Jeremiah 31:3), and also: "You are precious in my eyes and glorious, and . . . I love you" (Isaiah 43:4).

There is an axiom which maintains that we cannot love someone we do not know, nor can we know a person to whom we have not listened. Similarly, we must listen to God to know him before we can love him.

# Wonder and Reverence of the Lord

The theme for this week's prayer is admirably set by St. Paul when he declares: "How deep are the riches and the wisdom and the knowledge of God! How inscrutable his judgments, how unsearchable his ways!" (Romans 11:33). As we reflect on God's creative power, on his redemptive mercy and his providential care, we must stand in awe and wonder. It is impossible for the human mind to grasp this great God of love. Perhaps that is what inspired the psalmist to say: "God is great!"

### First Day—Psalm 91
We are assured of God's protection and see the pathos of a God waiting—and longing—to be asked.

### Second Day—Sirach 16:22-17:27
We see God's divine wisdom in creation, as well as his almighty power.

### Third Day—Psalm 84
God is everywhere, but he consecrates certain places where we can feel his presence more intimately.

### Fourth Day—Ephesiar.s 1:1-14
"Praised be the God and Father of our Lord . . ." for all he has done for us in Jesus.

### Fifth Day—Psalm 145
"His greatness is unsearchable." Our lives give testimony to the unending stream of divine love.

### Sixth Day—Psalm 147
God knows the myriad stars, not a sparrow falls without his knowledge: the hairs of our head are numbered. He does not want us to play God, but simply to wait on his love.

### Seventh Day—Psalm 149
God is praised by the whole of creation, but he especially wants praise from his people.

# God Loves Me

As we pray certain passages from the Old Testament, we become more and more aware of how much God really loves us. We need to know that God loves us, because many of us do not love ourselves. We know ourselves deep down inside. We are aware of our weaknesses, our selfishness, our failures, our sinfulness. Knowing ourselves, we wonder how God could really love us.

As we pray with Scripture, we become more and more convinced of God's overwhelming love. Even if our motives are often self-centered, God says, "I love you." In spite of our sinfulness, God still says, "I love you no matter what you've done." Regardless of our failure to reach the plateau of perfection that we have set for ourselves, God continues to love us with an everlasting love.

A basic step to prayer is this conviction that God loves us with an infinite love and that nothing we do can change that love. We must come to know him as a loving, kind, forgiving Father who welcomes his errant children with open arms.

When we are convinced that we are loved, only then can we be open and honest. There is no reason for pretense or sham. When we know that we are accepted, we need not wear any masks, or do any play acting. We can live in freedom and sincerity.

A consciousness of God's great love for us can lead us into greater depths of prayer. Deeply aware of his loving presence we want to whisper in the quiet of our hearts : "I love you, too" or "Thank you, Father, for your loving life in me, for your abiding presence sanctifying me at every moment of the day."

As we experience his loving presence within us, we will no longer require words or thoughts. We simply rest in his presence. We are aware of God as known and loved at the very core of our being.

# Listen to God Say, "I Love You"

God is not someone who is far away, nor is he an inexorable judge eager to punish us for our failures. No, he is a Father who loves us more than we could ask to be loved. God, the creator of the universe, the person who made all things out of nothing, loves us. He wants to care for us, share his divine life with us, and bring us to a perfect union with him for all eternity.

This truth is basic to our whole spiritual growth. We know with our minds that God loves us, but we must also be convinced in our hearts so that we can respond to his great love. This conviction will be ours when we hear God himself telling us of his great love for us. Listen to his own words in this week's Scripture.

### First Day—Isaiah 43:1-5
"I have called you by name: you are mine. . . . you are precious in my eyes . . . I love you."

### Second Day—Psalm 139
"O Lord, . . . you understand my thoughts. . . . and rest your hand upon me."

### Third Day—Ezekiel 34:11-16
God's providential care: "I myself will pasture my sheep."

### Fourth Day—Isaiah 49:1-16 (especially verses 1-2 and 14-16)
"The Lord called me from birth. . . . I will never forget you."

### Fifth Day—Jeremiah 31:31-34
"I will be their God and they shall be my people."

### Sixth Day—Psalm 145
Greatness and goodness of God: "The Lord is near to all who call upon him. . . . He hears their cry and saves them."

### Seventh Day—John 3:16-18
"God so loved the world that he gave his only Son."

# WEEK 6

## No Greater Love

In the New Testament Jesus tells us frequently how much he loves each one of us. "As the Father has loved me, so I have loved you" (John 15:9). "There is no greater love than this: to lay down one's life for one's friends" (John 15:13).

In addition to telling us of his great love, Jesus demonstrated that love by his whole life and all that he did. He reached out in love to the wedding party at Cana and worked his first miracle (John 2:1-2). He hugged the leper (Luke 5:13). The sinful woman heard him say: "Your sins are forgiven" because of her great love (Luke 7:48). The Samaritan woman felt his loving acceptance of her in spite of her sinfulness, and she became an apostle of love for her own people (John 4:4-42).

The whole healing mission of Jesus gave evidence of his infinite love: "the blind recover their sight, cripples walk, lepers are cured, the deaf hear, dead men are rasied to life, and the poor have the good news preached to them" (Matthew 11:5).

Even his enemies felt the warmth of his redeeming love: "Father, forgive them; they do not know what they are doing" (Luke 23:34).

This kind of love is overwhelming. It is beyond our human comprehension. As we strive to fathom its immensity, we become more and more aware of the gravity of our infidelities. We see them as a rejection of God's love for us. Sin is saying "no" to love. However, there is no reason for us to lose hope. Love surmounts all our failures. God himself gives us that assurance: "I drew them with human cords, with bands of love; I fostered them like one who raises an infant to his cheeks" (Hosea 11:4).

# Listen to Jesus Say, "I Love You"

The Father loves us so much that he sent his only Son into the world to save us. He sent Jesus that we might have life and have it more abundantly—a life of eternal union with him.

Jesus loves us so very much that he laid down his life for us. Love seeks union with the beloved. For this reason Jesus did not want to leave us orphans, hence he is dwelling with each one of us in his glorified, risen life. He is present to us at every moment of the day. As he did for the two disciples, he is trying to explain his Word to us as we make our daily trek to Emmaus. May our hearts burn within us as he talks to us along the way.

**First Day—John 15:1-13**
"As the Father has loved me, so have I loved you. Live on in my love."

**Second Day—Matthew 6:25-34**
The loving providence of God our Father.

**Third Day—1 John 3:1-2**
"See what love the Father has bestowed on us. . . . we are God's children now."

**Fourth Day—Ephesians 2:1-10**
"Because of his great love for us, he brought us to life with Christ when we were dead in sin."

**Fifth Day—1 John 4:7-19**
"Perfect love casts out all fear."

**Sixth Day—Romans 8:28-39**
Hymn to God's love for us: "The love of God . . . comes to us in Christ Jesus, our Lord."

**Seventh Day—John 17:20-26**
Perfect love is union with God: "that they may be one, as we are one."

# WEEK 7

## Spiritual Energy

Praying with Scripture is a great source of vitality on our daily journey of life. On our pilgrimage to the Father, the road is often rough and rocky. At times the hills seem high and the valleys quite deep. How often we need to be reassured and encouraged! God's Word is a limitless fountain of inspiration, hope and encouragement as we trek along the road of life.

Here is just one instance of St. Paul telling us how valuable God's Word is during these days of our earthly exile: "Everything written before our times was written for our instruction that we might derive from the lessons of patience and the words of encouragement in the Scriptures" (Romans 15:4).

Life is plagued with so much decision-making. It is difficult to ascertain just what God wants of us in certain situations. There is no magic formula for receiving God's guidance, but we can be assured that God will give us direction if we listen to him each day as he speaks to us through his Word.

Again it is St. Paul who assures us that many of our needs will be met in God's Word. He writes: "All Scripture is inspired of God and is useful for teaching—for reproof, correction, and training in holiness so that the man of God may be fully competent and equipped for every good work" (2 Timothy 3:16-17).

A quiet time of listening is essential to our spiritual growth. As we listen, God assures us that he is aware of our every anxiety and worry. He knows full well the problems which perplex us. In his Sermon on the Mount, Jesus instructs us: "Your heavenly Father knows all that you need. Seek first his kingship over you, his way of holiness, and all these things will be given you besides" (Matthew 6:32-33). We seek his kingdom as we listen to his Word.

"Speak, Lord, for your servant is listening" (1 Samuel 3:9).

# Sinfulness of Mankind

In these readings, listen to God complain about the neglect and rejection he suffers from his people. Listen to God as he deplores man's sinfulness, but also hear him reach out to his people with a forgiving, compassionate love. Sin is a tragic rejection of God's love, but God is not a vengeful God. He is the Good Shepherd always in search of the lost sheep.

This is why we are able to sing in the liturgy of Holy Saturday: "O happy fault that merited such a Redeemer."

**First Day—Hosea 2:4-25**
God's search for sinners: "I will lead her into the desert and speak to her heart."

**Second Day—Ezekiel 16:1-63**
The allegory of unfaithful Israel. (This includes all of us.)

**Third Day—Hosea 11:1-11**
God complains over unfaithful Israel: "I fostered them like one who raises an infant to his cheek."

**Fourth Day—Romans 1:18-32**
A picture of a sinful and decadent culture—humanity without Christ.

**Fifth Day—Genesis 3:1-24**
The sins of all mankind represented in the sin of Adam and Eve. God calls: "Where are you?"

**Sixth Day—Psalm 50**
God complains about hypocritical worship: "Offer to God praise as your sacrifice."

**Seventh Day—Psalm 82**
Against social injustice: "Rise O God; judge the earth, for yours are all the nations."

# WEEK 8

## Transformation

The power of God's Word can effect within us a complete transformation. As we feed at the table of his Word, we will discover a change coming over us. Our thinking, our attitudes, our relationship to others, will gradually change. We may not even perceive the transformation taking place within us, but his Word is powerful and effective.

Daily we eat food to sustain our physical life. After we have enjoyed a good meal, we are not particularly aware of the food we have consumed. However, the food is being digested and assimilated, carrying strength to every part of our body. Nourishing food keeps our body healthy and vigorous.

Similarly, praying with Scripture matures us spiritually. St. Paul is quite imperative when he advises us to "acquire a fresh, spiritual way of thinking. You must put on that new man" (Ephesians 4:23-24). And again: "Your attitude must be that of Christ" (Philippians 2:5). And furthermore: "Do not conform yourselves to this age but be transformed by the renewal of your mind, so that you may judge what is God's will, what is good and pleasing and perfect" (Romans 12:2).

The Christian who wants to follow Christ more closely, who wants to reflect the peace and joy of Christ in his interpersonal relations, must come frequently, even daily, to the table of the Lord's Word to be filled and formed into a new man. Nowhere can we discover the mind of Christ more clearly than in his own Word.

Just as we take food several times a day rather than eat one huge meal every few days, so with God's Word we need to come daily to listen to what he is telling us.

"If you live in me, and my words stay a part of you, you may ask what you will—it will be done for you" (John 15:7).

# My Own Sinfulness

As we strive to draw near to God, we get a better insight into the tragedy of sin. We see our sins as a rejection of God's love. Sin is a refusal to respond to God's love for us. Insignificant creatures that we are, we dare to say "no" to God in whose power is every breath we draw.

God is such a mysterious God. In spite of our sinfulness he continues to say: "I love you no matter what you have done." Each time we fail, he loves forgiveness into us.

**First Day—Romans 7:13-25**
Paul's lament over his sinfulness: "What happens is that I do, not the good I will to do, but the evil I do not intend."

**Second Day—Psalm 38**
Prayer for sinners: "My iniquities have overwhelmed me."

**Third Day—Luke 14:16-24**
"I tell you that not one of those invited shall taste a morsel of my dinner."

**Fourth Day—Psalm 51**
"Thoroughly wash me from my guilt and of my sin cleanse me."

**Fifth Day—1 John 2:1-11**
"I am writing this to keep you from sin."

**Sixth Day—Matthew 22:1-14**
"My friend, . . . how is it you came in here not properly dressed?"

**Seventh Day—Galatians 5:13-26**
The unredeemed person versus the Spirit-filled person.

## Purification

The conversion which takes place within us as we pray with Scripture has a purifying effect upon us. As we ponder what God is saying to us, we soon perceive whether or not our mind is the same as Christ's mind. We discover whether or not we are seeing things through Jesus' eyes.

As we expose our thinking to his Word, a real cleaning process takes place within us. We see how much of our thinking might be rationalizing. If our attitudes are foreign to the dispositions of Christ, we become aware of this division. Perhaps we have been rather self-centered and myopic in our outlook. As we become transformed by his Word, our self-centeredness begins to fade and our vision takes on the cosmic vision of Christ.

As we faithfully pray each day, a revolution is underway within our being. Jesus alerted us to this conversion when he told us through his apostles: "You are clean already, thanks to the word I have spoken to you" (John 15:3).

The letter to the Hebrews does not mince words in telling us how effective God's word can be in our formation: "Indeed, God's word is living and effective, sharper than any two-edged sword. It penetrates and divides soul and spirit, joints and marrow; it judges the reflections and thoughts of the heart. Nothing is concealed from him; all lies bare and exposed to the eyes of him to whom we must render an account" (Hebrews 4:12-14).

A daily prayer time with Scripture is an effective way for us to permit the Holy Spirit to transform us into persons radiating and reflecting Christ. With St. Paul, we, too, can say: "The life I live now is not my own; Christ is living in me" (Galatians 2:20).

# God Always Forgives

To err is human, to forgive is divine. No matter how grossly we have sinned, God is always anxious and eager to forgive us. He assures us: "Though your sins be like scarlet, they may become white as snow; though they be crimson red, they may become white as wool" (Isaiah 1:18). And again he says to us sinners: "How could I give you up . . . or deliver you up. . . . My heart is overwhelmed, my pity stirred.. . . For I am God and not man" (Hosea 11:8-9).

This kind of loving forgiveness we cannot comprehend with our finite minds. Only love—Divine love—can continue to forgive in this manner.

**First Day—Joel 2:12-17**
"Return to me with your whole heart."

**Second Day—Luke 15:11-32**
"Father, I have sinned against God and against you; I no longer deserve to be called your son."

**Third Day—John 8:3-11**
"Nor do I condemn you. . . . But from now on, avoid this sin."

**Fourth Day—Jeremiah 32:36-41**
"Into their hearts I will put the fear of me, that they may never depart from me."

**Fifth Day—Mark 2:1-12**
The faith of the companions elicits the forgiveness of Jesus: "My son, your sins are forgiven you."

**Sixth Day—John 10:1-18**
The Good Shepherd: "I came that they might have life and have it to the full."

**Seventh Day—Luke 15:1-7**
"There will likewise be more joy in heaven over one repentant sinner than over ninety-nine righteous people who have no need to repent."

# WEEK 10

## Scripture and Eucharist

The risen glorified Jesus is present among us in many different ways. He is not only present in Scripture, but he is the very Word of God. His unique presence in his Word is a mysterious presence beyond our rational understanding.

We may compare Scripture to the sacrament of the Eucharist, for it contains not only Jesus' Word, but also his very presence. As we receive him in daily Holy Communion, he nourishes and strengthens us, giving us the spiritual vitality and energy we need for each day's duties. Even more, his presence with us and within us gives us the assurance that we are not walking the road of life alone, but he is our constant companion. Each time we receive him at the eucharistic banquet, he shares anew with us his divine life.

As we pray with Scripture each day, Jesus personally comes to us to renew and implement his presence within us. Like Holy Communion, each day's prayer brings us new life, a new hope and encouragement. As we eat at the table of his Word we are nourished with a deeper, fuller life.

God invites us to the banquet of his Word: "Come to me heedfully; listen, that you may have life. . . . So shall my word be, that goes forth from my mouth; it shall not return to me void, but shall do my will, achieving the end for which I sent it" (Isaiah 55:3-11).

The Church has blended these two sources of spiritual growth admirably in the Liturgy of the Word and the Liturgy of the Eucharist in the Holy Sacrifice of the Mass. Each day we are nurtured by his Word and nourished by his sacramental presence. Such is the providence of our God!

# God's Mercy and Compassion

Our past sins are often a source of concern and worry. The devil will use all his diabolical ruses to keep us in a state of doubt and anxiety about the sins of our past life. We need to know with our hearts that God is a loving, kind and compassionate Father. We must be reassured that his mercy knows no bounds. Through the words of Scripture, God assures each one of us personally of his loving mercy. Listen to his own words as he speaks to our hearts.

**First Day—Sirach 18:1-13**
Divine mercy: "The Lord is patient with men and showers upon them his mercy."

**Second Day—Psalm 51**
"Have mercy on me, O God, in your goodness."

**Third Day—Hebrews 10:1-18**
"By this 'will,' we have been sanctified, through the offering of the body of Jesus Christ once and for all."

**Fourth Day—Isaiah 1:16-18**
"Though your sins be like scarlet, they may become as white as snow."

**Fifth Day—Ezekiel 36:25-27**
"I will sprinkle clean water upon you to cleanse you."

**Sixth Day—Luke 7:36-50**
"Your faith has been your salvation. Now go in peace."

**Seventh Day—John 21:15-17**
Jesus forgives Peter: "Do you love me?"

## Jesus Prayed

Jesus taught us to pray by both his instruction and his example. Our Lord rose early in the morning to have time for prayer. "Rising early the next morning, he went off to a lonely place in the desert; there he was absorbed in prayer" (Mark 1:35). He also prayed at night: "Then he went out to the mountain to pray, spending the night in communion with God" (Luke 6:12).

Jesus prayed before all the important decisions and events of his life, before choosing the twelve, and in the Garden of Gethsemane before his bitter passion and death.

Praising God is the highest form of prayer, and it is the one form least used by Christians. Again Jesus taught us the importance of praise as he prayed: "At that moment Jesus rejoiced in the Holy Spirit and said: 'I offer you praise, O Father, Lord of heaven and earth, because what you have hidden from the learned and the clever you have revealed to the merest children' " (Luke 10:21).

Jesus prayed always and everywhere. He prayed liturgically with his people. He prayed contemplatively. He prayed on location.

Our Lord used the Scriptures frequently in his teaching. He cited the prophets to prove his mission and his identity. Many times he explained that he was doing certain things to fulfill the Scriptures: "Today this Scripture passage is fulfilled . . ." (Luke 4:21).

Jesus also used the words of Scriptures as his prayer. After the Last Supper he sang the accustomed Passover psalms with his apostles. "Then, after singing songs of praise, they walked out to the Mount of Olives" (Matthew 26:30).

Two other instances of Jesus praying the Scriptures were on the cross. He was praying a portion of Psalm 31 when he prayed: "Father into your hands I commend my spirit" (Luke 23:46). Again when he pleaded, "I am thirsty" (John 19:28), he was praying Psalm 22.

With the disciples let us plead: "Lord, teach us to pray."

# "Give Thanks to the Lord"

We know from personal experience how pleased we are when someone is grateful for what we do. God, our Father, is likewise pleased when we, his children, turn to him with grateful hearts. When we express our gratitude, it enriches our own life and makes us even more aware of God's goodness to us.

When we ponder all that God is doing for us, we are compelled with the psalmist to say in awe: "How shall I make a return to the Lord for all the good he has done for me?" (Psalm 116:12).

**First Day—Ephesians 1:3-10**
We are God's adopted sons: "Praised be the God and Father of our Lord Jesus Christ, who bestowed on us in Christ every spiritual blessing."

**Second Day—Psalm 100**
"Give thanks to him; bless his name, for he is good."

**Third Day—Luke 17:11-19**
A portrait of ingratitude: "Were not all ten made whole? Where are the other nine?"

**Fourth Day— 1 Thessalonians 5:16-18**
Paul's admonition: "Render constant thanks."

**Fifth Day—Matthew 15:32-38**
Jesus gives us an example: "After giving thanks. . . ."

**Sixth Day—Psalm 147**
Grateful praise to the Lord: "Sing to the Lord with thanksgiving."

**Seventh Day—1 Timothy 2:1-4**
"I urge that . . . thanksgiving be offered for all men."

## Joy

The whole Christian era was inaugurated on a note of joy. When the angels announced to the shepherds that Jesus was born in Bethlehem, they underscored what effects this should have on the world: "I come to proclaim good news to you—tidings of great joy to be shared by the whole people" (Luke 2:10). Even today our materialistic world pauses each year to be joyous during the Christmas season.

Jesus himself informs us of the effect his Word should have upon us. As we pray Scripture we will experience a real interior joy unlike any joy we may have previously experienced. Jesus is the Word. He came to reveal the message of the Father. This is the Good News, and this is the source of our joy. Jesus himself told us the purpose of his teaching: "All this I tell you that my joy may be yours and that your joy may be complete" (John 15:11).

Later on the beloved apostle John explained what and why he wrote: "What we have seen and heard we proclaim in turn to you so that you may share life with us. . . . Indeed our purpose in writing you this is that our joy may be complete" (1 John 1:3-4).

St. Paul singled out joy as a special fruit of the Holy Spirit. "In contrast, the fruit of the Spirit is love, joy, peace . . ." (Galatians 5:22).

Paul also explains what our Christian life is all about: "The kingdom of God is not a matter of eating and drinking but of justice, peace and the joy that is given by the Holy Spirit" (Romans 14:17).

As we pray with Scripture, we, too, will experience the joy which the Good News can bring us. Filled with the Lord's joy, we can become apostles of joy to all those who traverse our path each day.

# God Promises Us a Redeemer

God's response to man's disobedience was an immediate manifestation of his infinite compassion. Even as he was calling to Adam after his sin—"Where are you?"—God was promising him a redeemer.

Throughout the ages the prophets repeatedly assured the chosen people that God would be faithful to his promise. For generations men longed for, prayed for, and waited for this event which would change the whole course of human history.

We, too, ought to pray for a fuller and deeper realization of what the Incarnation means to us. God is not only with us, but within us.

### First Day—Genesis 3:14-15
First promise of a redeemer: "He will strike at your head."

### Second Day—Isaiah 7:10-15
"The Virgin shall be with child, and bear a son, and shall name him Immanuel [God-with-us]."

### Third Day—Micah 5:1-4
"But you, Bethlehem . . . from you shall come forth for me one who is to be ruler in Israel."

### Fourth Day—Isaiah 9:1-6
"His dominion is vast and forever peaceful."

### Fifth Day—Isaiah 11:1-9
"A shoot shall sprout from the stump of Jesse and from his roots a bud shall blossom."

### Sixth Day—Isaiah 52:13-53:12
The suffering servant: "He shall take away the sins of many, and win pardon for their offenses."

### Seventh Day—Isaiah 40:1-5
Promise of the Messiah: "Make straight in the wasteland a highway for our God."

## Praying with the Heart

The Second Vatican Council, under the direction of the Holy Spirit, set in motion a spiritual renewal program which is reaching out in many directions. One aspect of the spiritual renewal is the upsurge of interest in all forms of prayer. Christians are no longer satisfied in merely "saying prayers," but are turning to higher forms of contemplative prayer.

For a long time we thought of contemplative prayer as the special prerogative of the great mystics, and perhaps those persons hidden in contemplative convents or monasteries. We excused ourselves from this form of prayer as impossible for anyone in normal life.

However, the Holy Spirit through the Vatican Council and other means has insisted that all men are called to holiness, meaning a deeper union with God through love expressed in prayer. The fifth chapter of the Constitution of the Church is entitled "The Universal Call to Holiness in the Church." As the title suggests, this call includes everyone regardless of each individual's walk of life.

It is stated thus in the chapter: "The Lord Jesus, the divine Teacher and Model of all perfection, preached holiness of life to each and every one of His disciples of every condition. He himself stands as the author and consummator of this holiness of life: 'Be you therefore perfect, even as your heavenly Father is perfect'. Indeed He sent the Holy Spirit upon all men that He might move them inwardly to love God with their whole heart and their whole souls, with all their mind and strength, and that they might love each other as Christ loves them" (Par. 40).

Genuine prayer is loving. As we come to God in prayer, especially contemplative prayer, we learn to love more deeply.

# God's Plan of Salvation Begins to Unfold

After generations of longing, waiting and praying for the coming of the Messiah, God's divine plan for the salvation of mankind begins to unfold. As usual, God's ways are not man's ways. God confirms this through his prophet Isaiah: "For my thoughts are not your thoughts, nor are your ways my ways" (Isaiah 55:8).

In preparing for the incarnation of his Son, God again does the unusual. Thus he proves to our hesitant hearts that these events are possible only by the power of God in our midst. In our prayer we discover the extraordinary means which God uses to effect his saving acts among us. Similarly, God works in the lives of all of us, as we step out in faith and permit him to work his wonders.

**First Day—Isaiah 2:2-5**
"Come, let us climb the Lord's mountain . . . that he may instruct us."

**Second Day—Luke 1:5-24**
Announcement of the birth of John the Baptist: "Joy and gladness will be yours."

**Third Day—Luke 1:26-38**
Mary's receptivity: "I am the servant of the Lord."

**Fourth Day—Luke 1:39-45**
The Visitation: "Elizabeth was filled with the Holy Spirit."

**Fifth Day—Matthew 1:18-24**
"Joseph, son of David, have no fear about taking Mary as your wife."

**Sixth Day—Luke 1:57-66**
The birth of John: "He began to speak in praise of God."

**Seventh Day—Luke 1:67-80**
Zechariah's song: "To guide our feet into the way of peace."

## Wordless Prayer

In the first document which issued from the Second Vatican Council—The Constitution on the Liturgy—we find various notions of contemplative prayer suggested. We find such expressions as: "the faithful" (i.e. all of us) are to "taste to their full" of the Paschal Mysteries and are to "be set on fire" by the Eucharist (Par. 10). This terminology is the same as that used in speaking of the higher forms of prayer.

Likewise in the Constitution on Divine Revelation, the Council Fathers assure us that "the believers," by praying with the Word of God, will grow in understanding of divine revelation "through the intimate understanding of the spiritual things they experience." Intimate understanding and the experience of spiritual things comes to us in contemplative prayer.

In contemplative prayer we experience a real sense of God's presence. We long to be alone with him. We experience God's love overwhelming us and quietly in our own hearts we strive to respond to his great love for us.

Contemplation is difficult to define since it is a personal experience of God which cannot be verbalized. We simply want to bask in God's presence. We want to be exclusively for God, and we want him to be for us.

In contemplative prayer Jesus makes his presence known within us. It is a mysterious presence, which assures us of his love. Love seeks union with the one loved. It experiences that union either in thought, when two people are separated from each other, or in personal presence to each other. This is the kind of union which we seek in contemplative prayer.

# God Prepares the World

Advent is a time of hopeful expectancy. It recalls the long years in which the Israelites waited, hoped and prayed for the coming of the Messiah.

Each day should be a time of expectancy for us as we await his manifestation in our daily living. Our prayer life depends upon our openness to God through our poverty of spirit. Mary teaches us this poverty in her beautiful song, the Magnificat.

**First Day—Luke 1:46-55**
"God who is mighty has done great things for me."

**Second Day—Jeremiah 1:4-10**
"Before I formed you in the womb I knew you."

**Third Day—Titus 2:11-14**
In preparation for the Lord's coming we must give up everything that does not lead to God.

**Fourth Day—Hebrews 1:1-9**
"Let all the angels of God worship him."

**Fifth Day—Acts 13:22-25**
"God has brought forth . . . Jesus, a savior for Israel."

**Sixth Day—Titus 3:4-7**
"When the kindness and love of God our savior appeared."

**Seventh Day—Hebrews 10:5-10**
"On coming into the world, Jesus said . . . I have come to do your will, O God."

## Meditation

How does contemplative prayer differ from meditation? When we spend time in meditation we approach our prayer more from the intellectual point of view, while contemplative prayer is more the "heart approach."

In meditation we recall some mystery of our faith, or some historical event of the life of Christ, or some truth or fact of God's dealing with his people. As we ponder this event, we try to understand something of God's love which prompts him to be so gracious with us. As we spend some time in reflection and consideration, we strive to understand what meaning this mystery has in our life. We strive furthermore to draw some conclusions or resolutions as guidelines for our daily living.

For example, if I meditate on the parable of the prodigal son, I have the assurance that God is a loving, merciful Father who is ever willing and eager to forgive me. I can resolve never to fear his punishments, but to come without hesitation to beg his mercy and forgiveness. Daily, this resolution gives me the assurance that God loves me and is anxious to forgive me regardless of how I might have fallen.

In meditation, there is a great deal of self-effort. Our prayer frequently is self-made prayer. This kind of prayer is fruitful and conducive to bringing us closer to God and also in preparing the way for contemplative prayer.

Meditation is prayer with the mind, while contemplation is prayer with the heart.

# The Word Was Made Flesh

"When peaceful stillness compassed everything and the night in its swift course was half spent" (Wisdom 18:14), God faithful to his promises sent his divine Son into human history. The Incarnation was the greatest event of human history. Yet God's ways are not our ways. Even though he is King of the universe, his throne was a manger, his palace a stable, his welcoming committee poor, hardworking shepherds. The chorus of angels added the only celestial touch.

"Yes, God so loved the world that he gave his only Son" (John 3:16). Rather, God loved me so much that he was incarnated into my life. All that God asks of me is a response to his great love.

**First Day—Luke 2:1-7**
   The birth of Jesus: "There was no room for them in the place where travellers lodged."

**Second Day—Wisdom 18:14-16**
   "When peaceful stillness compassed everything. . . ."

**Third Day—Luke 2:8-20**
   "Tidings of great joy to be shared by the whole people."

**Fourth Day—Matthew 2:1-12**
   "We have observed his star at its rising."

**Fifth Day—John 1:1-18**
   "The Word became flesh and made his dwelling among us."

**Sixth Day—Philippians 2:5-11**
   "He emptied himself and took the form of a slave."

**Seventh Day— 1 John 1:1-4**
   "We speak of the word of life."

## Affective Prayer

When we strive to pray contemplatively we strive to recall God's presence in us. We strive to make ourselves present to God. The purpose of contemplation is to unite ourselves with God. This is particularly the work of the Holy Spirit.

We sit at Jesus' feet, hear his words, experience his presence with us, then we speak quietly to him in our heart. This kind of prayer is a friendly and frequent conversation with him who loves us. We do not form the words with our lips, but only in our hearts.

In the first stage of contemplation we make acts of the will expressing our love in response to the overwhelming love which God is pouring out upon us. With our hearts we may say: "Thank you, Jesus" or "Jesus, I love you." When we realize that God has first loved us, perhaps our response may be: "I love you, too."

A person who was making a contemplative retreat once told me: "After two days of trying to pray contemplatively I have come two million light years closer to Jesus. Now I love him in a much deeper way and I know that he loves me."

This expression of our love and gratitude in our hearts is called affective prayer and is the first step into contemplation.

# Jesus, a Sign of Contradiction

Jesus drew the line very clearly when he said: ''He who is not with me is against me'' (Matthew 12:30). Both acceptance and rejection were the lot of Jesus from his birth. The shepherds, the wise men, all those who were awaiting the salvation of Israel, were jubilant at the tidings of great joy.

Simultaneously, the ugly monster of jealousy and intrigue, personified in King Herod, was raising its head. Jesus, even as an infant, was a threat to him. Yes, ''To his own he came, yet his own did not accept him'' (John 1:11).

In our prayer, let us discern how wholehearted is our daily acceptance of him in whatever manner he may come to us.

**First Day—Luke 2:21**
Jesus submits to the Law: ''The name Jesus was given the child.''

**Second Day—Philippians 2:5-11**
''It was thus he humbled himself. . . .''

**Third Day—Luke 2:22-35**
Simeon's faithfulness is rewarded.

**Fourth Day—Luke 2:36-38**
''She was constantly in the temple, worshipping day and night in fasting and prayer.''

**Fifth Day—Matthew 2:13-15**
''Take the child and his mother and flee to Egypt.''

**Sixth Day—Matthew 2:16-18**
The blood of martyrs is the seed of Christianity: ''A cry was heard at Ramah.''

**Seventh Day—Matthew 2:19-23**
''He shall be called a Nazarene.''

## Prayer Model

Jesus taught us how to pray both by word and by example. Lest his example seem too lofty for us to attain, he gave us a model of prayer in a creature like ourselves—his mother and ours.

The first requirement for prayer is a relationship with God. As we establish a relationship with God, we are praying. Words are a means of communication which strengthens and solidifies an established relationship. The relationship is all important.

On the human level we might draw an analogy from a mother-infant relationship. The mother and infant form a mutual relationship long before there is any verbal communication. After several years, this relationship of love is expanded and strengthened through verbal communication.

From the very moment of her conception, Mary had a deep relationship with God since she was conceived free from all sinfulness and all wrongful desires. As she grew, the awareness of God's presence actualized within her and she responded progressively until that momentous day when the angel Gabriel appeared to invite her into a unique and deeper relationship with God. Mary's exemption from all sin made her loving *fiat* to the redemption and to her divine motherhood possible.

We might say that Mary's value system changed as God called her into a more intimate relationship with him. Mary had eyes only for God.

The same is true of us. The closer we come to God, the more completely we give ourselves to him, the more radically will our value system change. What seemed important to us at one time in life may now have little or no importance.

This relationship with God is fundamental to a life of prayer.

# Desert Experience

When Jesus was baptized, the Father presented him as the Son of God and commissioned him for his messianic mission. The fact that Jesus was then tempted makes it perfectly clear that he is fully human too.

Jesus relived the experience of the Israelites in the desert. He thus taught us that each one of us will also have our desert experience.

Jesus showed us by his life and death that trials, temptations and suffering are our lot in life, and that through them we shall be made perfect. He would say to us: Be calm but vigilant.

**First Day—Luke 3:21-22**
The Father shows approval of Jesus: "Jesus was at prayer after likewise being baptized."

**Second Day—Luke 4:1-13**
Jesus perfected himself through the experience of every temptation.

**Third Day—James 1:12-15**
The value of perseverance: "Once he has been proved, he will receive the crown of life."

**Fourth Day—1 Peter 1:3-9**
"You may for a time have to suffer the distress of many trials."

**Fifth Day—John 15:1-3**
The vinedresser: "The fruitful ones he trims clean to increase their yield."

**Sixth Day—1 Peter 5:5-11**
"Your opponent the devil is prowling like a roaring lion."

**Seventh Day—2 Corinthians 12:7-9**
"For in weakness power reaches perfection."

## Public Prayer

Mary teaches us several kinds of prayer. Each method of prayer is conducive to an integrated prayer life. First of all, Mary prayed publicly with the others. She went regularly to the temple to pray. Mary and Joseph took the child Jesus to the temple to present him to the Lord. At this time they were active participants in the ceremony of purification. Yes, Mary prayed as she offered her son to God.

Twelve years later we find Mary going regularly to the temple. "His parents used to go every year to Jerusalem for the feast of the Passover and when he was twelve they went up for the celebration as was their custom" (Luke 2:41).

As the pilgrims marched to Jerusalem they prayed and sang. When the holy city came into view they sang the customary psalms more fervently. Surely Mary's heart sang the praises of God as she rejoiced with her people.

In the temple worship she prayed the ritual prayers along with many of the psalms which every good Jew knew by heart.

It does not take much of a stretch of the imagination to conclude that the holy family gathered regularly for prayer in that little sanctuary at Nazareth. How they must have pondered and discussed the Word of God!

Mary's participation in public worship is an example for us. As we join the people of God in public worship we are praising and thanking God for all that he is in our lives. Like Mary, our participation will be a source of faith and encouragement to others.

# Jesus Calls Us to Discipleship

At the beginning of his public life Jesus invites his disciples to "Come follow me." Only after he has taught and formed them does he give them the commission, "Go, therefore, and make disciples of all nations" (Matthew 28:19).

Jesus invites us to "come by yourselves to an out-of-the-way place and rest a little" (Mark 6:31). He invites us to follow him, work with him, walk with him, live with him. He makes us co-responsible with him. Enjoy victory with him. Celebrate with him.

**First Day—John 1:35-51**
Jesus invites you to be a disciple: "Come, see for yourself."

**Second Day—Luke 5:27-32**
"I have not come to invite the self-righteous to a change of heart, but sinners."

**Third Day—Matthew 11:28-30**
"Come to me, all you who are weary."

**Fourth Day—Ephesians 1:3-22**
Your call: "In him we were chosen."

**Fifth Day—Luke 5:1-11**
Our unworthiness is no factor in God's call.

**Sixth Day—John 15:9-17**
God's predetermined plan: "It was I who chose you."

**Seventh Day—Philippians 3:7-21**
We respond by detaching ourselves from all else: "For his sake I have forfeited everything."

# WEEK 19

## Communal Prayer

Mary prayed spontaneously with others. When Mary went to visit her cousin, "Elizabeth was filled with the Holy Spirit and cried out in a loud voice: Blest are you among women and blest is the fruit of your womb. But who am I that the mother of my Lord should come to me?" (Luke 1:41-43).

Mary responded to this spontaneous prayer of Elizabeth with that magnificent canticle which is repeated thousands of times each day around the world: "My being proclaims the greatness of the Lord, my spirit finds joy in God my savior . . ." (Luke 1:46-47).

Prayer from the heart comes naturally as we come closer to God. Our heart, like Mary's, simply bursts forth in praise and thanksgiving to God. I am certain that Mary's spontaneous prayers were frequent and fervent in the quiet of that home at Nazareth.

Luke is careful to point out Mary's presence in the upper room after the ascension of Jesus into heaven. There she prayed fervently with the special friends of Jesus. "Together they devoted themselves to constant prayer. There were some women in their company, and Mary, the mother of Jesus, and his brothers" (Acts 1:14).

How ardently Mary must have prayed with them! She knew from deep personal experience the power of the presence of the Holy Spirit within her. She knew, too, that the Holy Spirit could mold this motley group into a loving messianic community. She prayed also that they be granted the gifts of wisdom, knowledge and understanding so that they could become the pillars of that kingdom which her son had established in time and space.

Mary is our example of a communal or shared prayer which is becoming more customary today. Already it is binding many people with bonds of love and forming them into a genuine Christian community.

# Jesus' Healing Ministry

Jesus came into the world as a healer. He wanted to bring wholeness to everyone in need because he loves every person with an infinite love. "The healthy do not need a doctor; sick people do" (Luke 5:31). Jesus healed in every conceivable area: spiritual, psychological, physical. The healing mission of Jesus continues in the Church today, not only through the healing sacraments, but also through each one of us. We bring his healing to others in many different ways.

**First Day—Matthew 11:2-6**
Healing is a sign of Jesus' messiahship: "Go back and report to John what you see and hear."

**Second Day—Mark 6:7-13, 30-33**
"They . . . anointed the sick with oil, and worked many cures."

**Third Day—Mark 2:1-12**
Jesus cured the paralytic because of the faith of the community: "Jesus saw their faith."

**Fourth Day—Ezekiel 36:25-28**
Jesus fulfills this prophecy: "I will give you a new heart and place a new spirit within you."

**Fifth Day—James 5:14-16**
Jesus perpetuates his healing mission through us: "Pray for one another that you may find healing."

**Sixth Day—Mark 10:46-52**
The blind man tells Jesus, "I want to see." Jesus replies, "Your faith has healed you."

**Seventh Day—Matthew 8:5-13**
"It shall be done because you trusted."

# WEEK 20

## Meditation

Mary is our model of meditative prayer. In meditation we apply our minds to the magnificent mysteries of God's love. We try to understand the divine designs in order to be moved to love and gratitude. Through this rational process we draw conclusions as norms for our daily living with God.

Mary practiced this type of prayer also. When the shepherds came to the hillside stable and found their Savior enthroned in a manger, they "returned, glorifying and praising God for all they had heard and seen in accord with what had been told them" (Luke 2:20). In the meantime, "Mary treasured all these things and reflected on them in her heart" (Luke 2:19).

As Mary meditated upon these events, the mysterious designs of God began to unravel themselves to her. This was the fruit of her meditation.

The evangelist relates for posterity another example of Mary's meditative prayer. When Jesus was lost in the temple at the age of twelve, Mary and Joseph spent three agonizing days searching for him. "On the third day they came upon him in the temple sitting in the midst of the teachers, listening to them and asking them questions. All who heard him were amazed at his intelligence and his answers" (Luke 2:46-47).

"When his mother asked him: 'Son, why have you done this to us? . . .' He said to them: 'Why did you search for me? Did you not know I had to be in my Father's house?' But they did not grasp what he said to them" (Luke 26:48-50).

How true of us! How often we do not understand God's plan. God's ways are not our ways, nor his thoughts our thoughts.

"His mother meanwhile kept all these things in memory" (Luke 2:51). Yes, she meditated upon these events to help her understand how she could better fit into God's plans of salvation.

# Bond of Perfection

Jesus came into the world to teach us in concrete terms that God is a personal God who loves. Jesus reached out in love to everyone—to those who accepted his love, and to those who rejected the love he offered. He taught us that the most important commandment was to love. Jesus knew that this would be a difficult law; hence he led us gradually from the first to the fourth level of love.

**First Day—Luke 19:1-10**
Jesus teaches us to lead in loving: "Zacchaeus . . . I mean to stay at your house today."

**Second Day—Luke 10:25-37**
First level—Love your neighbor as yourself: "Do this and you shall live."

**Third Day—Matthew 25:31-46**
Second level—Love your neighbor as you love me: "As often as you did it for one of my least brothers, you did it to me."

**Fourth Day—John 15:12-17**
Third Level—Love one another as I have loved you: "There is no greater love than this: to lay down one's life for one's friends."

**Fifth Day—John 17:20-26**
Fourth Level—Union with God: "That they may be one, as we are one, I living in them, you living in me."

**Sixth Day—Revelation 2:1-7**
Love is a first priority: "You have turned aside from your early love."

**Seventh Day—Romans 5:1-11**
Jesus proves his love: "It is precisely in this that God proves his love for us. . . . "

## Contemplative Prayer

Private prayer is an aloneness with God. Much of our prayer time must be spent with God in the solitude of our hearts. Unless we first go to God in prayer to be nourished and fed by him, we will have very little to share with others. Here again Mary points the way by her own example.

Mary was a contemplative. Contemplative prayer is being alone with God, basking in the sunshine of his presence, feeling the warmth of his love for us. In this kind of prayer few, if any, words are required. At most what is called for is a quiet prayer in our heart such as: "My God, how great you are," or "I love you too, God," or "Thank you, Father." Contemplation is knowing at the core of our being that we are known and loved by God.

How happy Mary was to withdraw into the solitude of that sanctified home at Nazareth to be alone with her God. There she experienced his presence in her Son. Years later when she realized that Jesus was one with the Father, she understood that the Father, too, dwelt in that humble abode of the backward village. She understood, too, the presence of the Holy Spirit already at work in her, every day of her life.

Her hours of contemplation must have been many and frequent. They were hours filled with love, peace and joy. Mary's every heartbeat was in union with God. Her spoken words in Scripture are few indeed. Likewise her prayer for the most part must have been wordless. Words are not necessary when heart speaks to heart.

"Whenever you pray, go to your room, close the door, and pray to your Father in private" (Matthew 6:6).

# Jesus and Women

Jesus always came to the rescue of the downtrodden, the persecuted, the underprivileged. In his day women had few rights and little social standing. For this reason Jesus always went out to them with loving concern. He always defended women. He never permitted them to be criticized. He helped and healed them at every turn of the road. Jesus is the same yesterday, today and forever. In prayer, let us make his mentality our own.

**First Day—John 2:1-12**
Jesus' loving concern for a bride: "Do whatever he tells you."

**Second Day—John 8:2-11**
Jesus shows loving forgiveness toward an adulteress: "Nor do I condemn you."

**Third Day—Luke 10:38-42**
Martha and Mary: "Mary has chosen the better portion."

**Fourth Day—John 4:4-42**
The Samaritan woman at the well: "If only you recognized God's gift."

**Fifth Day—Luke 7:36-50**
A penitent woman: "Little is forgiven the one whose love is small."

**Sixth Day—Mark 5:21-43**
Jesus heals two women: "Fear is useless. What is needed is trust."

**Seventh Day—Luke 7:11-17**
The widow's son: "Jesus gave him back to his mother."

# WEEK 22

## Praying with Scripture

A method of prayer which is growing in popularity is praying with Scripture. This kind of prayer is listening with our hearts as we read God's Word. God's Word forms and molds us. It inspires, consoles, and strengthens us.

Mary prayed the Scriptures. Here again she can teach us by her example. Each year Mary and Joseph went up to the temple for the feast of the Passover. Here they read the Scriptures, prayed and sang the psalms.

Without any stretch of the imagination, we can visualize Mary, Joseph and Jesus pondering and praying the Word of God in that little home at Nazareth.

When Mary poured forth her joy in Elizabeth's home, she gave evidence of her acquaintance with Scripture. Her song reflects the same joy which issued from the heart of Hannah many years earlier when she presented her son, Samuel, to the Lord.

Jesus himself gives witness to his mother's praying and living the Word of God. One day, as he was teaching, a woman wanted to compliment him so she called out: "Blest is the womb that bore you and the breasts that nursed you." Jesus must have smiled his approval of this praise of his mother, but he replied in effect that his mother was blest not merely because she gave him physical birth. No, he said: "Rather . . . blest are they who hear the Word of God and keep it" (Luke 11:27-28).

In effect Jesus was saying that his mother was truly blessed because she knew the Word of God and put it into practice in her life, permitting his Word to form and mold her.

"Happy is the man who reads this prophetic message, and happy are those who hear it and heed what is written in it, for the appointed time is near" (Revelation 1:3).

# "Lord, Teach Us to Pray"

Jesus prayed! He sought out lonely spots for his prayer, in a desert, on a mountain top, in an olive grove. He prayed early in the morning (Mark 1:35). He prayed at night. In fact he frequently spent the whole night in prayer (Luke 6:12). He also went regularly to the synagogue "as he was in the habit of doing" (Luke 4:16). He taught us how to pray by instruction and by his example. With his disciples let us sit at the feet of the Master and plead: "Lord, teach us to pray."

**First Day—Matthew 6:5-13**
"Pray to your Father in private."

**Second Day—Matthew 7:7-11**
The effectiveness of our prayers: "Ask and you shall receive."

**Third Day—Luke 11:5-13**
"How much more will the heavenly Father give the Holy Spirit to those who ask him."

**Fourth Day—Matthew 18:19-20**
Communal prayer: "Where two or three are gathered in my name, there am I in their midst."

**Fifth Day—John 14:12-14**
"Whatever you ask in my name, I will do."

**Sixth Day—Mark 11:15-25**
"If you are ready to believe that you will receive whatever you ask for in prayer, it shall be done for you."

**Seventh Day—James 1:5-8**
"Let him ask it from the God who gives generously."

## Faith—A Prayer Posture

Prayer must begin, continue and end with a deep abiding faith. Faith characterized Mary's whole life. Faith permeated her life of prayer.

When she was asked to accept the divine maternity, she did not hesitate, nor did she ask for any assurances. She asked only one question, and that was to ascertain just how God wanted to accomplish this tremendous mystery in her life. When the angel explained: "The Holy Spirit will come upon you and the power of the Most High will overshadow you" (Luke 1:35), it was then that Mary stepped out in faith. Even though nothing like this was ever heard of in the annals of history, yet Mary believed. She knew that nothing was impossible with God. Then came her faith with commitment and expectance: "I am the servant of the Lord. Let it be done to me as you say" (Luke 1:38).

At the outset of his public life, Jesus went to a wedding feast in Cana. It was here that Mary asked her son for his first miracle—so great was her faith. As the wine was running out, Mary said to her son: "They have no more wine" (John 2:3). Even though Jesus assured her that his hour had not yet come, she turned to those waiting on the table with expectant faith and advised them: "Do whatever he tells you" (John 2:5). That is faith.

There are different levels of faith: first, that kind of faith which accepts intellectually a revealed truth which cannot be understood; secondly, a faith that carries with it a commitment; thirdly, expectant faith.

Mary's was a confident faith of expectancy. She expected her Son to do something about the wine shortage, and he did.

As the poet Richard Crashaw puts it: "The modest water saw its God and blushed."

# Who Is Jesus?

"Who do people say that I am?" (Mark 8:27). For 2,000 years men have discussed that question in business, social, educational and religious circles. As in Jesus' day, a whole kaleidoscope of answers is offered.

Jesus becomes more personal when he asks, "And you, who do you say I am?" (Mark 8:29). Let him help us formulate our response to that query as he speaks to us through his Word:

**First Day—John 10:1-16**
   "I am the good shepherd."

**Second Day—John 8:12-20**
   "I am the light of the world."

**Third Day—John 14:6-7**
   "I am the way, and the truth and the life."

**Fourth Day—John 15:1-8**
   "I am the true vine."

**Fifth Day—John 6:35-40**
   "I myself am the bread of life."

**Sixth Day—Mark 14:60-65**
   " 'Are you the Messiah, the Son of the Blessed One?' . . . 'I am.' "

**Seventh Day—John 11:1-44**
   "I am the resurrection and the life."

# WEEK 24

## Poverty of Spirit—A Prayer Posture

As we come to prayer our attitude is all important. Our prayer posture must be one of total dependence upon God. We must come to prayer with a poverty of spirit, recognizing our own inability even to pray. St. Paul assures us: "The Spirit too helps us in our weakness, for we do not know how to pray as we ought; but the Spirit himself makes intercession for us with groanings that cannot be expressed in speech. He who searches hearts knows what the Spirit means, for the Spirit intercedes for the saints as God himself wills" (Romans 8:26-27).

A humble disposition is essential for prayer. Recall the story Jesus told about the Pharisee and the tax collector who went to the temple to pray (Luke 18:9-14). The tax collector "went home from the temple justified but the other did not." It was the humility of the tax collector which was pleasing to God. Then Jesus concluded: "For everyone who exalts himself shall be humbled while he who humbles himself shall be exalted."

Our Blessed Mother came to prayer with genuine humility. This was her constant prayer posture. She knew her own lowliness and attributed everything to God:

"My being proclaims the greatness of the Lord,
    my spirit finds joy in God my savior.
For he has looked upon his servant in her lowliness;
    all ages to come shall call me blessed.
God who is mighty has done great things for me,
    holy is his name."

(Luke 1:46-49)

Mary prayed with humility because she was always aware that everything which was happening in her and through her was taking place by the power of God. Humility must characterize our prayer life if it is to be pleasing to God.

# The Teaching Ministry of Jesus

As we contemplate the mystery of Jesus, we can learn from his response to every situation in life. As he teaches his disciples on every occasion, let us be present with him, listen intently to his words, see the reaction on the faces of his hearers.

As we do so, we will gradually put on a new man, one formed anew in the image of his Creator.

**First Day—Matthew 14:22-36**
Jesus tests the faith of his disciples: "It is I. Do not be afraid! . . . How little faith you have."

**Second Day—Matthew 16:13-23**
"And you, who do you say I am?"

**Third Day—Matthew 18:1-14**
"Unless you change and become like little children."

**Fourth Day—Mark 10:13-16**
Jesus and little children: "Let the children come to me and do not hinder them."

**Fifth Day—Matthew 20:20-27**
"The Son of Man who has come, not to be served by others, but to serve."

**Sixth Day—Matthew 21:18-32**
"You will receive all that you pray for, provided you have faith."

**Seventh Day—Luke 19:1-10**
"The Son of Man has come to search out and save what is lost."

## Yes, Lord

Jesus taught us to pray "Thy will be done." An acquiescence to God's will is an essential prayer posture. We must not only accept God's will, but we must also have a deep desire to do his will always, even if it leads us through the valley of suffering.

Mary's whole life was one continual "yes" to God, even in privation and suffering. Her acceptance without a word of complaint of the poverty of Bethlehem, the exile in Egypt, the injustice of Calvary, manifests her prayerful attitude of obedience to God.

Her heart was always in tune with God's will. This is prayer. When Simeon told Mary, "You yourself shall be pierced with a sword," she quietly accepted that destiny (Luke 2:35).

In one brief statement, without adjective or adverb, John describes Mary's posture of acquiescence on the height of Calvary. "Near the cross of Jesus there stood his mother" (John 19:25). This laconic statement is filled with pathos, but it also says much about Mary's prayer life. Her heart was united with her Son's and thus in union with the will of the Father. Mary did not threaten the executioners; she did not scream at the terrible mockery of justice. No, she "stood." She had united her sacrifice in union with that of Jesus. This was all incorporated in her eternal *fiat*.

Long hours of being alone with God in prayer had taught her how unsearchable are his ways and how unfathomable are his plans.

# Rejection

At every turn of the road, Jesus experiences rejection. He is hated by his enemies, avoided by many, considered mad by his relatives. He reaches out in love, only to be rejected. This is the paradox of the gospel message. Jesus himself warned: "They will harry you as they harried me" (John 15:20). Paul prepared us for this rejection as followers of Jesus: "The message of the cross is complete absurdity to those who are headed for ruin, but to us who are experiencing salvation, it is the power of God" (1 Corinthians 1:18). Contemplative listening means that we feel, taste and experience all these rejections with the risen and glorified Jesus.

**First Day—Matthew 2:13-23**
"Herod is searching for the child to destroy him."

**Second Day—Luke 4:14-30**
"They rose up and expelled him from the town."

**Third Day—John 6:60-71**
"Many of his disciples broke away and would not remain in his company any longer."

**Fourth Day—Matthew 19:16-30**
"The young man went away sad."

**Fifth Day—John 1:10-16**
"His own did not accept him."

**Sixth Day—Mark 3:20-30**
"He is out of his mind."

**Seventh Day—Mark 12:1-12**
"The stone rejected by the builders. . . ."

# WEEK 26

## In Jesus' Name

Jesus is the master teacher. He taught us how to pray. He advises us to ask in his name. "Whatever you ask the Father he will give you in my name" (John 16:23). And again he tells us: "Anything you ask in my name I will do" (John 14:14).

This is an important requisite for prayer. However, we must understand what Jesus meant. Much more is involved than merely using the formula "in the name of Jesus."

In Hebrew thought, the name of a person stood for the whole person. To pray in the name of Jesus means to pray in the person of Jesus—to pray as Jesus would have prayed. This means that we see people and situations as Jesus does.

To pray in the name of Jesus means that we must have the mind and heart of Jesus. We must put on the mind which was in Christ Jesus. In other words our prayer should be only what Jesus seeks and wants. Our thoughts, hopes and desires should be perfectly in accord with the mind of Christ. When we cultivate this attitude, then we speak with the power and authority of Jesus.

St. Paul teaches us that our mentality must be the same as the mind of Jesus. "Your attitude must be that of Christ" (Philippians 2:5). Again he says: "Acquire a fresh spiritual way of thinking. You must put on that new man" (Ephesians 4:23-24).

Asking the Father for anything in Jesus' name means more than merely a formula. When our thinking is in tune with Jesus, then our prayer will be pleasing to God and will be granted for his honor and glory.

# The Washing of the Feet

The ministry of Jesus was a ministry of service. Part of that service was to cleanse us from our imperfections and purify us for our union with him. The washing of the feet was a purifying process as a preparation for the Holy Eucharist. It was a ministry of humble service. It was also a powerful example which Jesus held up for our emulation.

Genuine Christian joy comes not from receiving, but from giving, not so much from being served as from serving others.

**First Day—John 13:1-20**
Jesus gives us an example: "Do you understand what I just did for you?"

**Second Day—Matthew 18:1-14**
"Unless you change and become like little children, you will not enter the kingdom of God."

**Third Day—Philippians 2:5-11**
Jesus' humility: "Obediently accepting even death, death on a cross.'

**Fourth Day—1 Timothy 5:7-10**
An evaluation of Christian character: "Has she washed the feet of Christian visitors?"

**Fifth Day—John 10:14-18**
"I lay down my life."

**Sixth Day—Ephesians 5:1-7**
"He gave himself for us as an offering to God, a gift of pleasing fragrance."

**Seventh Day—Luke 22:24-30**
"I am in your midst as one who serves."

# WEEK 27

## A Sacrifice of Praise

The Holy Sacrifice of the Mass is a prayer par excellence. The entire Mass is offered to the Father in the name of Jesus, the principal high priest. As we unite ourselves with him, Christ offers the Mass as an infinite sacrifice in our name. It is a perfect prayer of praise and thanksgiving offered to the Father by Jesus in our name.

Almost all of the prayers at Mass end with a formula presenting our petition "Through Christ Our Lord" or one of many variants of this formula.

At the little elevation we pray: "Through him, with him, in him, in the unity of the Holy Spirit, all glory and honor is yours almighty Father, forever and ever."

The fact that Jesus is the principal offerer adds an infinite dimension to our prayer. We are not praying alone. We are not worshipping alone. We are presenting our praises, our thanksgiving and our intercessory prayer "through Jesus Christ Our Lord."

In Eucharistic Prayer IV we pray: "Lord, look upon this sacrifice which you have given to your Church; and by your Holy Spirit, gather all who share this bread and wine into the one body of Christ, a living sacrifice of praise." Our prayer life can become a living sacrifice of praise only if we pray in Jesus' name by the power of his Spirit.

"Through him let us continually offer God a sacrifice of praise, that is, the fruit of lips which acknowledge his name" (Hebrews 13:15).

# I Myself Am the Bread of Heaven

The heart of Calvary is suffering, rejection, obedience. The risen, glorified Jesus is present in us, his Body, as we relive Calvary each day.

Jesus gave us the Eucharist banquet to nourish and nurture us along the highway of life. He knew the hills and the valleys which would be our daily fare on our pilgrimage to the Father. He wants to be with us in all the vicissitudes of life. He is truly Viaticum, food for our journey. Jesus became Eucharist for us, so that we, in turn, could become Eucharist to others.

**First Day—Exodus 16:4-36**
"I will now rain down bread from heaven for you."

**Second Day—John 6:1-15**
"Jesus then took the loaves of bread, gave thanks, and passed them around to those reclining there."

**Third Day—John 6:25-59**
"I myself am the bread of life."

**Fourth Day—John 6:60-71**
The disciples find Jesus' words hard to accept: "Do you want to leave me too?"

**Fifth Day—Luke 22:7-20**
"I have greatly desired to eat this Passover with you before I suffer."

**Sixth Day—I Corinthians 11:17-34**
Paul's admonition on receiving the Eucharist: "A man should examine himself first. . . ."

**Seventh Day—Hebrew 9:11-28**
The sacrifice of Jesus: "How much more will the blood of Christ cleanse. . . . our consciences!"

## His Will

Jesus was always deeply concerned about doing the will of his Father. Repeatedly he told us that he had come to do what the Father asked of him. On one occasion he said: "Doing the will of him who sent me and bringing his work to completion is my food" (John 4:34). "As is written of me in the book, I have come to do your will, O God" (Hebrews 10:7).

This is an all-important attitude for us to adopt as we come to prayer. We must seek and do the will of God. Time spent in quiet reflection and meditation reveals to us what God wants of us. As we listen to his word we can more easily discern and discover what God is asking us to do. This is real prayer. It is sitting at the feet of Jesus and listening with our hearts to what he is saying to us.

The will of God for us is not always easy. On the contrary, it may cause a great deal of pain at times. Nevertheless as we spend time in prayer we find the strength to accept whatever his will is in our regard.

Here again, Our Lord gives us the example. In the Garden of Gethsemane, when the vision of all the suffering which lay ahead crushed Jesus to the ground, he prayed: "Father, if it is your will, take this cup from me; let not my will but yours be done." The evangelist goes on to say: "In his anguish he prayed with all the greater intensity" (Luke 22:42, 44).

We must come to prayer prepared to ask and accept the will of God in all things. In such a prayer there is real peace. When the will of God seems to crush us, we too must pray with even greater fervor. Therein we find strength and even joy.

# The Agony in the Garden

The anticipation of an unpleasant or painful experience is frequently worse than the experience itself. Jesus suffered the dreadful pain of anticipation in Gethsemane. In addition he foresaw the futility of so much of his pain. He knew the indifference, the ingratitude and the open hostility which he would have to suffer in his Body throughout the ages. This terrible pain made him cry out: "*Abba* (O Father), you have power to do all things. Take this cup away from me." Then came his magnificent resignation: "But let it be as you would have it, not as I" (Mark 14:36).

**First Day—Matthew 26:36-46**
Gethsemane: "My heart is nearly broken with sorrow."

**Second Day—John 12:23-28**
"It was for this that I came to this hour."

**Third Day—Hebrews 5:5-10**
"He learned obedience from what he suffered."

**Fourth Day—John 14:28-31**
"I go away for a while, and I come back to you."

**Fifth Day—Hebrews 4:14-16**
"We do not have a high priest who is unable to sympathize with our weakness."

**Sixth Day—Luke 22:47-53**
"Would you betray the Son of Man with a kiss?"

**Seventh Day—John 18:1-14**
Almighty power bound: "Who is it you want?"

## Let It Go

When we come to prayer we must turn everything over to God. We must be willing to let go before we can come before our Father in real prayer.

One time when I was leading a workshop on prayer, I asked the participants to share any prayer experience which they might have had or any prayer posture which they found helpful.

One man in his middle thirties shared this experience with us. "As a small boy, I lived on a farm and I was praying for a bicycle and a 22-rifle. I kept asking God for both those things which I wanted badly. God was not answering my prayer.

"Then one day I got a bright idea. I liked to fly my kite down by the river. The draft was always good there. It came to me that God was up in heaven and he could not hear my request. I got the idea that if I could put my request on the tail of my kite, I could fly my kite high and God could read my prayer.

"Having written a note to that effect, I went excitedly down to the river to fly my kite. The wind was just right and my kite went higher and higher. Finally, I came to the end of the string and the kite kept tugging on my hand just as a fish on the line. I looked up and could see that my kite was not high enough for God to see.

"I knew it would have to go up higher if God was going to see my prayer. I started to cry and cry because I loved my kite. Finally with tears streaming down my face I looked up into the heavens and I let my kite go.

"Ever since that day, when I come to God in prayer I let everything go. That's what God taught me that day many years ago."

# Jesus Rejected by His Own

Judas, motivated by avarice, succumbed to temptation. Jesus called him "friend" despite his act of perfidy, but Judas, filled with remorse and despair—could not turn to the outstretched arms of Jesus. He did not comprehend God's loving, merciful forgiveness. .

On the other hand, Peter boasted in his pride that he would never deny Jesus. Pride goes before the fall. Yet unlike Judas, Peter's pride evaporated into humility. Sorrow, not remorse, flooded his heart. He became the lovable penitent Peter.

**First Day—Luke 22:1-6**
The plot to arrest Jesus: "They were delighted, and agreed to give him money."

**Second Day—John 13:18-30**
"I tell you solemnly one of you will betray me."

**Third Day—Matthew 27:3-10**
Judas feels remorse not sorrow: "I did wrong to deliver up an innocent man."

**Fourth Day—Luke 22:31-38**
"Simon, Simon! Remember that Satan has asked for you."

**Fifth Day—Matthew 26:69-75**
Peter betrays the Lord: "I do not even know the man."

**Sixth Day—Luke 22:61-62**
Sorrow not remorse: "The Lord turned around and looked at Peter."

**Seventh Day—Acts 10:34-43**
A repentant Peter carries on the mission of Jesus: "He commissioned us to preach to the people."

## Pray Always

Prayer is by no means limited to words only. In fact words are rather poor vehicles for our thoughts and feelings. An old axiom has it: "Actions speak louder than words."

Our actions too are prayers. When our activities are in harmony with what God wants of us at a particular time, and when they are offered in union with Jesus, then they become prayer. God is pleased with this attitude of prayerfulness.

St. Paul encourages us to express our gratitude to God by our actions. "Whatever you do whether in speech or in action, do it in the name of the Lord Jesus. Give thanks to God the Father through him" (Colossians 3:17). In another letter he says: "The fact is that whether you eat or drink—whatever you do—you should do all for the glory of God" (1 Corinthians 10:31).

Jesus also taught us that our good deeds were not only prayer for us, but they could even lead others to prayer. "Your light must shine before men so that they may see your goodness in your acts and give praise to your heavenly Father" (Matthew 5:16).

In the story of the last judgment, Jesus told us how he would consider actions such as feeding the hungry and giving drink to the thirsty, if they were done with the proper motive. "I assure you, as often as you did it for one of my least brothers, you did it for me" (Matthew 25:40).

Scripture also tells us: "Prayer and fasting are good, but better than either is almsgiving accompanied by righteousness" (Tobit 12:8).

# Trial And Condemnation

Jesus did not defend himself before the Sanhedrin, Herod or Pilate. He did not try to justify his teachings or actions because he saw the futility of such an attempt in this farce of adjudication. Also, Jesus was "guilty" because "The Lord laid upon him the guilt of us all" (Isaiah 53:6). Such is God's magnanimity!

**First Day—Matthew 26:57-68**
Before the Sanhedrin, "Jesus remained silent."

**Second Day—John 18:19-24**
Jesus asks Annas, "Why do you question me?"

**Third Day—John 18:28-40**
Pilate: "I find no case against this man."

**Fourth Day—Luke 23:1-12**
Herod questions Jesus, but "Jesus made no answer."

**Fifth Day—John 19:1-16**
Pilate's attempt to release Jesus: "Look at the man!"

**Sixth Day—Matthew 27:27-31**
"All hail, king of the Jews!"

**Seventh Day—Luke 23:26-31**
Via Dolorosa: "They put a crossbeam on Simon's shoulders."

## Discipleship

Activity can be prayer provided that it is activity begun in prayer, motivated by prayer, performed as a prayer of love. Jesus lived a very active life for three years. However, all his activity was interspersed with prayer. He prayed before all the important events in his life—before choosing the apostles, before raising Lazarus, in the Garden of Gethsemane, on the Cross.

The activities of our life must be frequently punctuated with times of prayer. Our prayer will then give the proper direction to our action. Jesus said: "Unless the grain of wheat falls to the earth and dies, it remains only a grain of wheat" (John 12:24). This attitude of mind is foreign to our human nature; hence the need for the proper formation of attitude in prayer.

Jesus laid down a condition for discipleship when he said: "Whoever wishes to be my follower must deny his very self, take up his cross each day, and follow in my steps" (Luke 9:23).

This condition for discipleship requires time spent in daily prayerful reflection to remind us that all our activity must be supported by prayer. A cross is formed when our will runs perpendicular to God's will; prayer alone can bend our will to run parallel with the will of our loving Father. This is what Jesus taught us by his example of frequently setting aside time for prayer, whether by rising early in the morning long before dawn, or by spending the whole night in prayer.

Again, we say: Lord, teach us to pray by making all our daily activities a living sacrifice of praise.

# Death By Crucifixion

Crucifixion was the most shameful and also the most painful type of execution known in Jesus' day. How better could Jesus prove his love! To what further extent could he make his sacrifice complete!

Even on his pain-released deathbed, Jesus' ministry of love continues to the thief, to his mother, to his executioners, to all mankind.

**First Day—Luke 23:39-43**
The repentance of the criminal: "This day you will be with me in paradise."

**Second Day—Luke 23:32-37**
"Father forgive them: they do not know what they are doing."

**Third Day—John 19:25-30**
"Near the cross of Jesus there stood his Mother."

**Fourth Day—Psalm 22**
"My God, my God, why have you forsaken me?"

**Fifth Day—Isaiah 52:13-53:12**
"It was our infirmities that he bore, our sufferings that he endured."

**Sixth Day—Hebrews 10:1-18**
"By one offering he has forever perfected those who are being sanctified."

**Seventh Day—Mark 8:34-38**
"Take up his cross, and follow in my steps."

# WEEK 32

## Intercessory Prayer

The most common form of prayer is intercessory prayer or prayers of petition. This is the most frequently used type of prayer. Many people rarely use any other form of prayer. It is certainly good prayer, but it is not the highest form of prayer.

God does want us to come to him with our needs. Prayer of this kind does remind us that of ourselves we can do nothing, but that with God's help all things are possible.

Prayer is the key to the Father's heart. People of prayer are invincible. They are not conquered by the evil one, by any resistance, by any suffering or difficulty in life. Prayer is the surest weapon for victory. People of prayer are always happy people.

Now the important question is how are we to use this most powerful gift which God has given us. Jesus said: "Ask and you shall receive" (John 16:24). Thus Jesus promises that help will come to him who asks. The important thing is that we must ask in the right way.

Prayer in itself does not bring God's help. Only the right prayers are answered. This is a basic biblical truth. God commits himself to his word only when what we ask is in harmony with his will.

It is important that we learn how we are to pray, and in which situation the various kinds of prayer should be used. No school is as effective as the school of experience.

"Lord, teach us to pray" (Luke 11:1).

# He Is Risen

He is risen! For Jesus—What a triumph! What a victory! For us—What joy! What peace! Christ has paid the penalty of sin. He has conquered death. Taste victory with him. Rejoice with him. Joyfully let the alleluias resound in your heart.

**First Day—Matthew 28:1-10**
"He is not here. He has been raised, exactly as he promised."

**Second Day—John 20:1-10**
"Then the disciple who had arrived first at the tomb went in. He saw and believed."

**Third Day—Romans 6:3-11**
"If we have been united with him through likeness to his death, so shall we be through a like resurrection."

**Fourth Day—Acts 2:29-36**
"This is the Jesus God has raised up, and we are his witnesses."

**Fifth Day—Colossians 3:1-11**
"Be intent on the things above."

**Sixth Day—1 Corinthians 15:20-28**
"In Christ all will come to life again."

**Seventh Day— 1 Corinthians 15:35-58**
"The last Adam has become a life-giving spirit."

## Childlike Prayer

Repeatedly Jesus assures us: "Unless you change and become like little children, you will not enter the kingdom of God" (Matthew 18:3). This pertains in a special way to our prayer. The Father's heart is open to all his children's needs. Little ones conquer the Father's heart by their childlike attitude. Children come before their father with confidence and love and trust and lay their smallest needs before him. We must do the same with God. This pleases him very much since we come in all simplicity and in loving trust.

Jesus, speaking of a human father, says: "If you, with all your sin, know how to give your children what is good, how much more will your heavenly Father give good things to anyone who asks him!" (Matthew 7:11).

When we come to the Father in a childlike attitude of love and confidence, our prayer is pleasing to him. If our request conforms to his will, he will grant it, and at times with surprising rapidity and generosity.

It may be that he will hold back the answer to a prayer if there is a specific obstacle hindering the one praying, such as a resentment or an unforgiving heart. In doing this, the Father is teaching us so that later he may give us even more.

We may be poor and may have needs simply because we are not childlike in approaching the Father. "You do not obtain because you do not ask" (James 4:2).

# Appearances

By his death and rising Jesus is able to share his divine life with us. He is living with us and within us. We are Christians not because we follow a certain moral code, believe a set of doctrines, or worship in a particular way. No, we are Christians because of Christ's indwelling. He called us to a magnificent vocation when he invited us to baptism. Through baptism he invited us into his family, the people of God. He adopted us as his children. This gives us our real dignity as a person and as a Christian.

**First Day—John 20:11-18**
Mary Magdalene: "I have seen the Lord!"

**Second Day—Song of Songs 3:1-4**
"I found him whom my heart loves."

**Third Day—Mark 10:46-52**
Eyes of faith: "Rabboni, . . . I want to see."

**Fourth Day—1 John 5:1-13**
"Whoever possesses the Son possesses life."

**Fifth Day—John 12:23-36**
I—once I am lifted up from earth—will draw all men to myself."

**Sixth Day—1 Peter 3:13-22**
"You are now saved by a baptismal bath."

**Seventh Day—Ephesians 1:15-23**
"May the God of our Lord Jesus Christ . . . grant you a spirit of wisdom and insight to know him clearly."

## Obstacles to Prayer

Holy Scripture clearly mentions obstacles to prayer. "Lo, the hand of the Lord is not too short to save, nor his ear too dull to hear. Rather, it is your crimes that separate you from God, it is your sins that make him hide his face so that he will not hear you" (Isaiah 59:1-2).

One attitude which deals a death blow to our prayer is the attitude of pride and self-righteousness. Perhaps a person who is wealthy and well satisfied does not find himself in a situation where he has to come to the Father to ask for anything. Perhaps he is talented and does not feel any need for God's help. He may claim to be a self-made man who does not have to rely on any one, not even on God. Such an attitude is tragic. It will soon lead to misery and unhappiness.

God wants us to come as little children to him again and again because he is our Father and like any Father, he enjoys doing good and giving us his gifts.

"On that day you will ask in my name and I do not say that I will petition the Father for you. The Father already loves you, because you have loved me" (John 16:26-27).

# Down The Road to Emmaus

Daily we walk the road to Emmaus. It is our daily trek down the highway of life. Jesus did not leave us orphans, but he is with us at every moment of our pilgrimage back to the Father. Do we recognize him? It was only after their invitation to have Jesus stay with them that the disciples recognized him. Do we invite him daily into our lives, our homes our activities?

**First Day—Luke 24:13-35**
The road to Emmaus: "Stay with us. It is nearly evening."

**Second Day—Luke 18:31-34**
Jesus warned his disciples of the fate awaiting him in Jerusalem, but "they understood nothing of this."

**Third Day—1 Peter 1:3-12**
"There is cause for rejoicing here."

**Fourth Day—Luke 9:18-22**
"The Son of Man . . . must first endure many sufferings."

**Fifth Day—Acts 2:22-38**
"For it was impossible that death should keep its hold on him."

**Sixth Day—Isaiah 54:4-10**
"Your redeemer is the Holy One of Israel, called God of all the earth."

**Seventh Day—Luke 2:25-38**
"For my eyes have witnessed your saving deed."

## Hindrances to Prayer

The New Testament mentions several sins which are obstacles to prayer. This means that there are definite prerequisites for prayer. If these are not fulfilled, our prayer will be impeded to say the least.

Above all this includes the transgressions against the Ten Commandments. In general some of these are first a refusal to forgive. "If you do not forgive others, neither will your Father forgive you" (Matthew 6:15).

Another gross impediment to our prayers is anger and dissension. Paul advises his protege Timothy: "It is my wish, then, that in every place the men shall offer prayers with blameless hands held aloft, and free from anger and dissension" (1 Timothy 2:8).

St. Peter also gives us some paternal advice about prayer: "Treat women with respect as the weaker sex, heirs just as much as you to the gracious gift of life. If you do so, nothing will keep your prayers from being answered" (1 Peter 3:7).

The same apostle encourages us to step out in faith and remove all mistrust and fears from our heart as we come to prayer. "Therefore do not be perturbed; remain calm so that you will be able to pray. Above all, let your love for one another be constant, for love covers a multitude of sins" (1 Peter 4:7-8).

Greed and avarice are obstacles to God's response to our prayer. Jesus said: "Give, and it shall be given to you. Good measure pressed down, shaken together, running over, will they pour into the fold of your garment. For the measure you measure with will be measured back to you" (Luke 6:38).

# Jesus Appears to His Disciples

Jesus appeared to his disciples on many occasions and at odd times. He did so to assure them that he was alive and to strengthen their faith. Experience the presence of the risen Jesus with you and within you. Feel his love warming and enveloping you. Respond to his love with: "I love you, too!"

**First Day—John 20:19-23**
An unannounced visitor: "Peace be with you."

**Second Day—John 14:27-31**
"My peace is my gift to you."

**Third Day—John 20:24-29**
"Do not persist in your unbelief, but believe!"

**Fourth Day— 1 John 1:1-5**
"What we have seen and heard we proclaim in turn to you so that you may share life."

**Fifth Day—John 4:46-54**
"The man put his trust in the word Jesus spoke to him."

**Sixth Day—Acts 3:22-26**
"All the prophets . . . have announced the events of these days."

**Seventh Day—Luke 24:36-46**
"Look at my hands and feet."

# Roadblock to Effective Prayer

The beloved apostle assures us that a clear conscience is a prerequisite for an answer to prayer. He writes: "Beloved, if our consciences have nothing to charge us with, we can be sure that God is with us and that we will receive at this hands whatever we ask" (1 John 3:21-22).

The psalmist, too, assures us that God will answer the prayers of the just: "Turn from evil and do good; seek peace, and follow after it. The Lord has eyes for the just and ears for their cry" (Psalm 34:15-16).

These words may cause us some concern. Who of us can claim such holiness that God will hear our prayer? God's Word does not mean that only people who have never sinned will be heard. No, it is impossible for us mortals to live without sinning. Our human nature is too prone to sin.

Scripture is speaking about the sinner who is willing to turn from his sinful ways. A decisive obstacle to answered prayer is unrepented sins to which a person clings. When sin is forgiven we can pray with a humble and repentant heart. The promise Jesus made concerning the tax-collector is a promise to all of us. "The other man, however, kept his distance, not even daring to raise his eyes to heaven. All he did was beat his breast and say, 'O God, be merciful to me, a sinner.' Believe me, this man went home from the temple justified but the other did not. For everyone who exalts himself shall be humbled while he who humbles himself shall be exalted" (Luke 18:13-14).

# Jesus Appears in Galilee

Jesus held out such great hope to us when he said: "I am the resurrection and the life: whoever believes in me, though he should die, will come to life" (John 11:25-26). This truth is the source of our hope and joy. What peace it brings to our heart as we daily progress toward our own resurrection.

Be for God, and let God be for you. Relax in his presence and rejoice with him in his resurrection and the promise it gives us.

**First Day—John 21:1-14**
"It is the Lord!"

**Second Day—John 21:15-19**
"Do you love me?" "Lord, you know everything. You know well that I love you."

**Third Day—Luke 5:1-11**
Jesus calls his first disciples: "Leave me, Lord. I am a sinful man."

**Fourth Day—Luke 22:31-36**
"I have prayed for you that your faith may never fail."

**Fifth Day—Matthew 16:13-20**
"I will entrust to you the keys of the kingdom of heaven."

**Sixth Day—2 Peter 1:12-19**
In this letter, we see Peter "feeding" the Lord's people: "I intend to recall these things to you constantly."

**Seventh Day—Acts 20:28-38**
"Keep watch over yourselves, and over the whole flock."

## "Not of This World"

A materialistic attitude is a gross obstacle to prayer. The philosophy of materialism makes man a little god. Its criteria of success are fame and fortune. A man is esteemed or respected only by what he has accomplished or by the fortune he has amassed. There is no place for God in this mentality.

It is obvious that this attitude is not conducive to genuine prayer. Jesus says: "Seek first his kingship over you, his way of holiness, and all these things will be given you besides" (Matthew 6:33). Jesus is assuring us that as we strive to grow in holiness everything else will be given to us without our asking.

Jesus also warns us about seeking only material success and possessions. "What profit would a man show if he were to gain the whole world and destroy himself in the process? What can a man offer in exchange for his very self?" (Matthew 16:26).

Those who are imbued with a materialistic philosophy soon become enslaved by it. All their time and talent, their energy and their every waking hour, are consumed in pursuit of these neon-standards which are diametrically opposed to the standards given by Jesus.

Jesus gave us the Magna Carta of Christian living when he taught us the Beatitudes. These Beatitudes are just a further explanation of his admonition: "Seek first his kingship over you." This is an ideal prayer posture.

# He Went to Heaven

Having finished his ministry on earth, Jesus took leave of his disciples and ascended to his glory at the right hand of the Father. He continues his ministry in us and among us through the presence and the power of his Holy Spirit. The disciples realized this. Hence, at his departure they returned to Jerusalem "filled with joy" and not sadness.

**First Day—Acts 1:6-11**
"He was lifted up before their eyes."

**Second Day—Luke 24:50-53**
"They . . . returned to Jerusalem filled with joy."

**Third Day—Hebrews 10:11-14**
"Jesus . . . took his seat forever at the right hand of God."

**Fourth Day—Ephesians 2:1-10**
"God is rich in mercy. . . . and gave us a place in the heavens."

**Fifth Day—Psalm 68:16-19**
God's triumphal procession: "You have ascended on high."

**Sixth Day—Philippians 3:17-21**
"We have our citizenship in heaven."

**Seventh Day—Matthew 24:36-51**
Be watchful: "You cannot know the day your Lord is coming."

## Do Not Be Afraid

One of the essential attitudes of mind in coming before the Lord in prayer is an attitude of trust and confidence. We are God's children, and we come before him who is our loving and kind Father. In prayer there is no place for fear.

We are dominated by so many fears; fear of rejection, fear of failure, fear of our unworthiness in coming before God. Each time there is an encounter with the divine, there is also a quiet, reassuring caution not to be afraid. When the angel appeared to Mary, he said: "Do not fear, Mary" (Luke 1:30). To the shepherds the angel said: "You have nothing to fear!" (Luke 2:10). When Jesus was on his way to raise the daughter of Jairus, he said to the official: "Fear is useless. What is needed is trust" (Mark 5:36). When the apostles saw Jesus walking toward them on the water, they were terrified. "Jesus hastened to reassure them: 'Get hold of yourselves! It is I. Do not be afraid!'" (Matthew 14:27).

On another occasion Jesus assured us: "Do not let your hearts be troubled. Have faith in God and faith in me" (John 14:1).

If we truly love God, we will come to him in prayer with confidence and trust. He is a Father who wants to provide all that his children need. Jesus gently invites us: "Come to me, all of you who are weary and find life burdensome, and I will refresh you" (Matthew 11:28).

Furthermore, John tells us: "Love has no room for fear; rather, perfect love casts out all fear" (1 John 4:18).

Praying with genuine trust and confidence brings real peace and joy to our fearful hearts.

# Spirit of God in the Old Testament

The mystery of the Blessed Trinity is not clearly taught in the Old Testament. Nevertheless, the Spirit of God is operative in many different capacities. The Spirit is the source of the early prophecies. He is a creative Spirit. He is also the Spirit of unity and the builder of community. In this, as in so many ways, the Old Testament is the preparation for the outpouring of the Holy Spirit in these messianic days.

**First Day—Numbers 11:24-29**
"As the spirit came to rest on [the elders], they prophesied."

**Second Day—Isaiah 11:1-9**
A prophecy of Immanuel: "The spirit of the Lord shall rest upon him. . . ."

**Third Day—Isaiah 61G1-3**
"The spirit of the Lord God is upon me, because the Lord has anointed me."

**Fourth Day—Ezekiel 36:25-28**
"I will place a new spirit within you."

**Fifth Day—Ezekiel 37:1-14**
"I will . . . put my spirit in you that you may live."

**Sixth Day—Isaiah 44:3-4**
"I will pour out my spirit upon your offspring."

**Seventh Day—Joel 3:1-5a**
"I will pour out my spirit upon all mankind."

## Praise

We commonly make a distinction between prayers of praise, thanksgiving and petition. Many of us are accustomed to turn to God with prayers of petition. It is so natural to come to our loving Father with all our needs. This pleases God. As our Father, he is eager to help us his children.

Another form of prayer is the prayer of praise. This form of prayer does not come as easily to us as prayers of petition and thanksgiving.

In Scripture praise and thanksgiving are often united in the same movement of soul and found in the same text. For example: "I will give you thanks in the vast assembly, in the mighty throng I will praise you" (Psalm 35:18).

In Scripture, God is revealed as worthy of our praise because of all his marvelous gifts to us. As a result praise and thanksgiving are brought together in the same passages.

If we make a distinction between the forms of prayer, we can say that praise looks more to the person of God than to his gifts. Praise is more centered on the Lord himself, more deeply lost in God. It is closer to adoration.

When we praise God we are riveting our attention on God alone. When we praise God for his might and his mercy we are concentrating solely on God. Our interest is not divided. We are not asking for any help, or for an answer to a particular problem. God alone is the object of our prayer of praise.

God wants our praise. He himself tells us: "He that offers praise as a sacrifice glorifies me" (Psalm 50:23).

# Pentecost

True to his promise, Jesus did not leave us orphans, but sent the Holy Spirit. Pentecost marks the birthday of the Church. Like so many mysteries it is not a once-in-history event; the work of the Holy Spirit goes on daily in our lives. He is dwelling in us. We are his special temples.

**First Day—Acts 2:1-13**
"All were filled with the Holy Spirit."

**Second Day—Acts 2:14-36**
"He first received the promised Holy Spirit from the Father, then poured this Spirit out on us."

**Third Day—Acts 10:34-48**
"The Holy Spirit descended on all who were listening to Peter's message."

**Fourth Day—John 20:21-23**
"Receive the Holy Spirit."

**Fifth Day—Acts 8:14-17**
"The pair upon arriving imposed hands on them and they received the Holy Spirit."

**Sixth Day—Acts 19:1-7**
"Did you receive the Holy Spirit when you became believers?"

**Seventh Day—Acts 11:11-18**
"God has granted life-giving repentence even to the Gentiles."

## Person of Praise

To praise God for himself and his grandeur is the duty and privilege of every one of us. Praising God is the most effective way we can fulfill our obligation to love and serve him here in our earthly exile.

God wants us to praise and glorify him. Our hearts and our lips should ever be raised in praising him for what he is and what he is doing for us. We should praise him for his infinite goodness, for his inexhaustible patience, his compassionate mercy, his creative love, his providential care, his redeeming power. We should praise him for the love, peace and joy which he bestows upon us. There is no end to the litany because everything we are and have has come from God. As St. Paul exclaims: "How deep are the riches and the wisdom and the knowledge of God!" The psalmist admonishes us and encourages us to fulfill our duty of praise to God: "Offer to God praise as your sacrifice and fulfill your vows to the Most High" (Psalm 50:14). And again: "Praise the name of the Lord, for his name alone is exalted" (Psalm 148:13).

In other words as we strive to praise God for himself and all his magnificent works, we are fulfilling our prime duty as Christians.

"Come, let us sing joyfully to the Lord" (Psalm 95:1).

# Period of Preparation

Jesus carefully and meticulously prepared us for the work of the Holy Spirit in us, with us and through us. He not only promised us the Spirit, but he also explained that the Holy Spirit would teach us all things and would be our consoler and advocate. He would complete the work which Jesus had begun in us.

**First Day—Mark 1:7-12**
"He saw . . . the Spirit descending on him like a dove."

**Second Day—Luke 11:9-13**
The Father's gift: "Ask and you shall receive."

**Third Day—John 14:16-17**
The Father will send another Paraclete: "He remains with you and will be within you."

**Fourth Day—John 14:25-26**
"The Paraclete, the Holy Spirit . . . will instruct you in everything."

**Fifth Day—John 16:4b-16**
"Being the Spirit of truth he will guide you to all truth."

**Sixth Day—Acts 1:1-5**
"Wait . . . for the fulfillment of my Father's promise."

**Seventh Day—Acts 1:12-14**
"Together they devoted themselves to constant prayer."

## People Of Praise

God is calling us to become a people of praise. Through the prophet, God is telling us how much he wants to form us into a praising people.

"See, I am doing something new! . . .
For I put water in the desert
   and rivers in the wasteland
   for my chosen people to drink,
The people whom I formed for myself,
   that they might announce my praise" (Isaiah 43:19-21).

God is calling us to praise him constantly in the quiet of our heart. He is also calling us to announce his praise among our fellowmen, especially those with whom we live and move and have our being each day. He is calling us to raise our hearts and voices in praise of his divine majesty. This is what he means when he says that he is forming a people to announce his praise. The psalmist encourages us: "Sing to the Lord a new song of praise in the assembly of the faithful" (Psalm 149:1).

St. Paul also assures us that God is calling us together as a community to praise him. In writing to the Ephesians, St. Paul says ". . . that all might praise the glorious favor he has bestowed on us in his beloved." He continues: "He is the pledge of our inheritance, the first payment against the full redemption of a people God has made his own, to praise his glory" (Ephesians 1:6, 14).

Jesus formed his Church as a community. We, the Church, are fulfilling our mission most effectively as we become more and more a people of praise.

# Mystery of God's Presence in Us

God is dwelling in us through the power of his Holy Spirit. He called us by a special vocation at the time of our baptism. He adopted us as his sons and daughters. This gives us our real dignity as persons and as Christians. The abiding presence of the Holy Spirit within us is the source of our hope and joy. We are never alone. What peace, what consolation is ours!

**First Day—1 Corinthians 3:16-23**
"The Spirit of God dwells in you."

**Second Day—2 Corinthians 6:14-18**
"You are the temple of the living God."

**Third Day—1 Corinthians 6:12-19**
"Your body is a temple of the Holy Spirit, who is within."

**Fourth Day—Romans 5:3-11**
"The love of God has been poured out in our hearts through the Holy Spirit."

**Fifth Day—1 Corinthians 2:6-16**
"God revealed this wisdom to us through the Spirit."

**Sixth Day—2 Corinthians 3:1-18**
"Where the Spirit of the Lord is, there is freedom."

**Seventh Day—Colossians 2:6-15**
"God gave you new life in company with Christ."

## A Living Sacrifice of Praise

God is calling us and forming us into a people of praise. This formation takes place wondrously in the Holy Sacrifice of the Mass. When we come together to celebrate the Eucharistic Liturgy, God is drawing us closer together in a strong bond of unity. This is one of the powerful effects of the Mass.

Also, the Mass is the most perfect way to praise God. The Mass is a sacrifice of praise. We offer our meager praise through Jesus to the Father. This adds an infinite dimension to our prayer of praise. We are no longer striving to praise God ourselves, but in the Mass we are united with our eternal High Priest who makes our efforts a perfect hymn of praise.

We begin the Mass in a spirit of repentance. This repentance is necessary in order to praise God well. Perhaps we should first repent for failing to praise God to the extent to which he calls us.

In the Mass, we pray that through the power of the Holy Spirit we may be formed into a people of praise:

" . . . by your Holy Spirit, Father, all who share this bread and wine into the one body of Christ, a living sacrifice of praise" (Eucharistic Prayer IV).

St. Paul states so aptly what we accomplish through the Mass: "All praise to God, through Jesus Christ our Lord!" (Romans 7:25).

# Source of Power

Jesus told us in no uncertain terms that without him we could do nothing. For this reason he gave us his Holy Spirit as the source of our power and strength. The Holy Spirit gives us the power to live our life as true followers of Jesus. He also is the source of our power to bear witness to others. St. Paul says it well: "I work and struggle, impelled by that energy of his which is so powerful a force within me" (Colossians 1:29).

**First Day—Luke 24:46-49**
"Remain . . . until you are clothed with power from on high."

**Second Day—Acts 1:6-9**
"You will receive power when the Holy Spirit comes down on you; then you are to be my witnesses."

**Third Day—John 1:10-12**
"Any who did accept him, he empowered to become children of God."

**Fourth Day—Galatians 4:6-7**
"You are no longer a slave but a son!"

**Fifth Day—John 3:1-3**
"See what love the Father has bestowed on us in letting us be called children of God!"

**Sixth Day—Romans 15:7-13**
"Through the power of the Holy Spirit you may have hope in abundance."

**Seventh Day—1 Peter 4:7-11**
The Spirit gives us the power to love, and "love covers a multitude of sins."

## Our Calling

The author of the Book of Sirach teaches us that although our praise cannot adequately fulfill our obligation to worship God, it is still the highest and best form of prayer. He begs us to praise God who is so much greater than all his works—greater by far than we can ever imagine: ''Let us praise him more, since we cannot fathom him, for greater is he than all his works'' (Sirach 43:29).

He encourages us to continue to praise God even though we cannot fathom his infinity. When we reflect on God's greatness, his almighty power, his infinite love, we are simply overwhelmed and words fail us. Yet that should not deter us: ''Lift up your voices to glorify the Lord, though he is still beyond your power to praise'' (Sirach 43:31).

What we can see and imagine of God's infinity is very limited because our human comprehension cannot fathom God's immensity. Our minds cannot grasp the divine designs in everything about us regardless of how immense or how infinitesimal each thing is. However, Sirach urges us to continue our hymn of praise to God: ''For who can see him and describe him? or who can praise him as he is? Beyond these, many things lie hid; only a few of his works have we seen'' (43:33-34).

As we become a people of praise, the exciting joy of living and knowing the infinite grandeur and beauty of God will know no bounds.

# Gifts of the Spirit

The first and most important gift of the Holy Spirit is the gift of himself. He is dwelling within us. The spiritual gifts are the manifestation of God's presence and power within us. God endows us with certain gifts, not for ourselves, but always for the building up of his Body, the Church. The Holy Spirit can use anyone of us as his instrument, as an extension of his mission among men.

**First Day—Isaiah 11:1-3**
"The spirit of the Lord shall rest upon him."

**Second Day—1 Corinthians 12:1-6**
"There are different gifts but . . . the same God who accomplishes all of them in everyone."

**Third Day—1 Corinthians 12:7-11**
"To each person the manifestation of the Spirit is given for the common good."

**Fourth Day—1 Corinthians 12:12-31**
We have unity even in the diversity of our gifts: "All of us have been given to drink of the one Spirit."

**Fifth Day—1 Corinthians 13:1-13**
The greater gifts: "The greatest of these is love."

**Sixth Day—1 Corinthians 14:1-5**
"Set your heart on spiritual gifts—above all, the gift of prophecy."

**Seventh Day—1 Corinthians 14:6-12**
Instructions on the gift of tongues: "Since you have set your heart on spiritual gifts, try to be rich in those that build up the Church."

## Alleluia

One of the richest expressions of praise is the beautiful exclamation, "Alleluia." This exclamation is used extensively in all Christian worship, especially during the Easter season.

The word "Alleluia" is a compound word made up from several different words. It is derived from the Hebrew word 'hallel' which means to praise in song. The letter 'u' denotes the second person plural, while 'iah' is an abbreviation for the name of God—Yahweh, the Lord God.

Alleluia = Hallelu-Yah = Praise Yah (weh)

Alleluia is a word which introduces many of the psalms. "Alleluia! Praise the Lord all you nations" (Psalm 117). "Alleluia! Give thanks to the Lord for he is good" (Psalm 118).

St. John used this exclamation of praise in the Book of Revelation. For example in chapter nineteen we read: "Alleluia! Salvation, glory and might belong to our God" (v. 1). And again: "Once more they sang "Alleluia!" (v. 3). Again: "Alleluia! The Lord is King, our God, the Almighty!" (v. 6).

There are many popular chants being sung today using this striking exclamation of praise. We are beginning to use Alleluia more extensively as an ejaculation of praise to our loving and gracious God.

May our hearts ring constantly with:

ALLELUIA    ALLELUIA    ALLELUIA

# Function And Use of the Gifts

God calls each one of us to a specific role or ministry during our sojourn here on earth. Of ourselves we could never accomplish the task; hence he gives us the gifts necessary for our special work. Since these are gifts, they are freely given; God asks only that we be open to receive them. Furthermore they must be used only as God wills. As we ponder the wonders of God, we can say with the psalmist: "What is man that you should be mindful of him?" (Psalm 8:5).

**First Day—1 Corinthians 14:20-25**
God is truly among us.

**Second Day—Romans 12:3-8**
"We have gifts that differ according to the favor bestowed on each of us."

**Third Day—Ephesians 4:1-6**
"There is one body and one Spirit."

**Fourth Day—Ephesians 4:7-16**
"Each of us has received God's favor in the measure in which Christ bestows it."

**Fifth Day—1 Corinthians 14:26-40**
"Set your heart on prophecy . . . but make sure that everything is done properly and in order."

**Sixth Day—Titus 3:4-8**
"He saved us through the baptism of new birth and renewal by the Holy Spirit."

**Seventh Day—1 Peter 4:12-19**
The blessings of persecution: "Happy are you when you are insulted for the sake of Christ."

## God of Praise

In Scripture we find songs of praise bursting with enthusiasm, multiplying words in an attempt to describe God and his grandeur. These songs speak of God's greatness and goodness (Psalm 145), of his love and fidelity (Psalm 89), of his might (Psalm 29), of his wonderful plan (Isaiah 25), of his mighty deeds (Psalms 104 and 105).

From the works of God, we are brought back to their author, our loving and gracious Father. "Great is the Lord and highly to be praised!" (Psalm 145:3) "O Lord, my God, you are great indeed! You are clothed with majesty and glory" (Psalm 104:1).

These hymns of praise in Scripture also celebrate the great name of God. "Glorify the Lord with me, let us together extol his name" (Psalm 34:4). "I will extol you, O my God and King, and I will bless your name forever and ever" (Psalm 145:1). "O Lord, you are my God, I will extol you and praise your name" (Isaiah 25:1).

In the New Testament, the praise of God consists first of all of solemnly proclaiming his greatness. Here are some examples: "My being proclaims the greatness of the Lord" (Luke 1:46). "Therefore I will praise you among the Gentiles and I will sing to your name" (Romans 15:9). " . . . and every tongue proclaim to the glory of God the Father: Jesus Christ is Lord!" (Philippians 2:11).

These are but a few of the many verses in Scripture that proclaim praise to God and urge us to raise our voices to extol his name.

As we pray his Word daily, we will each be formed into a person of praise. As more and more of us learn to praise God, we will become a people of praise.

# The Fruit of the Spirit

By his presence and power within us, the Holy Spirit produces his fruit in us. This fruit is the most convincing sign of God's presence. It is our best witness. Jesus said: "You will know them by their deeds" (Matthew 7:16). In order to produce fruit, we must be receptive to what the Holy Spirit wants to accomplish in us. We must permit him to melt us, to mold us, and to use us as he wishes.

**First Day—Galatians 5:22-26**
"Since we live by the Spirit, let us follow the Spirit's lead."

**Second Day—Galatians 5:13-15**
Love: "Out of love, place yourself at one another's service."

**Third Day—Romans 14:17-19**
Joy: "The kingdom of God is . . . the joy that is given by the Holy Spirit."

**Fourth Day—Ephesians 2:12b-22**
Peace: "It is he who is our peace."

**Fifth Day—2 Timothy 2:1-7**
Patient endurance: "Bear hardship along with me as a good soldier of Christ Jesus."

**Sixth Day— 2 Timothy 2:22-26**
Kindness: "Be kindly toward all."

**Seventh Day—2 Corinthians 9:6-15**
Generosity: "Thanks be to God for his indescribable gift!"

## Thank You, Lord

Since God is so good to us, it is obvious that we must respond in gratitude for all his blessings. God does want our prayer of thanksgiving. He wants us to come to him with hearts filled with joy and gratitude.

We ourselves have need to express our gratitude. Psychologists tell us that nothing is really our own until we have expressed it in words. As we thank God in our prayer, our gratitude becomes more intense.

Jesus taught us by his own example that we must be grateful to God. Twice the evangelist tells us that Jesus gave thanks to his Father at the first multiplication of the loaves. "Jesus then took the loaves of bread, gave thanks, and passed them around to those reclining there. . . . near the place where they had eaten the bread after the Lord had given thanks" (John 6:11, 23). Jesus again gave thanks at the second multiplication of the loaves. "He took the seven loaves and the fish, and after giving thanks he broke and gave them to the disciples, who in turn gave them to the crowds" (Matthew 15:36).

Jesus did the same at the Last Supper. "Then, taking bread and giving thanks, he broke it and gave it to them, saying: "This is my body to be given for you" (Luke 22:19).

Jesus again gave thanks at the tomb of Lazarus before he restored Lazarus to life. Jesus prayed: "Father, I thank you for having heard me" (John 11:41).

By his example Jesus taught us how important it is to express our gratitude and appreciation to God daily for his countless benefactions.

"Let all your works give you thanks, O Lord, and all your faithful ones bless you" (Psalm 145:10).

# Walking in the Spirit

We are living in the age of the Spirit. The manifestation of his presence and power among us is quite evident in our times, especially since Vatican II. St. Paul advises us to be receptive to the Holy Spirit within us, to be docile to his inspiration and guidance, and to be generous in permitting him to give direction to our lives. In this there is true peace and joy.

**First Day—Hebrews 3:1-6**
"Christ was faithful as the Son placed over God's house."

**Second Day—Matthew 11:28-30**
"Learn from me, for I am gentle and humble of heart."

**Third Day—Ephesians 5:15-21**
"Keep careful watch over your conduct."

**Fourth Day—1 Thessalonians 5:16-22**
"Do not stifle the Spirit."

**Fifth Day—2 Timothy 1:6-14**
"I remind you to stir into flame the gift of God."

**Sixth Day—Ephesians 4:25-32**
"Do nothing to sadden the Holy Spirit."

**Seventh Day—Ephesians 6:18-20**
"At every opportunity pray in the Spirit."

## Sincerity

As creatures we have a solemn obligation to offer our thanks to God for his manifold blessings. He is loving life and breath into us at this very moment. Every heart beat is a special blessing from God.

Jesus taught us how important is our expression of gratitude to God. When he cured the ten lepers who came to him, only one returned to express his gratitude. Perhaps the other nine could have been excited and anxious to run home to their family and friends from whom they had been isolated for so long. Regardless of the reasons, Jesus expressed his disappointment. "Were not all ten made whole? Where are the other nine? Was there no one to return and give thanks to God except this foreigner?" (Luke 17:17-18).

Jesus also warned us against a false type of gratitude. God wants us to be sincere in thanking him. He does not want empty words. Jesus taught us a valuable lesson when he told us about the Pharisee and the tax collector who went down to the temple to pray (Luke 18:9-14). Jesus told us how futile was the prayer of the Pharisee, who gave thanks with his lips and not his heart: "I give you thanks, O God, that I am not like the rest of men—grasping, crooked, adulterous—or even like this tax collector." Jesus said of the difference of the prayer of these two men: "This man (the tax collector) went home from the temple justified but the other did not."

When we recognize our total dependence upon God and come to him with childlike thanks, he is pleased with our prayer of gratitude.

# Prayer Of Praise

The prayer of praise is the highest form of prayer. God is calling us, as he called his people in past generations, to become a people of praise—"The people whom I have formed for myself that they might announce my praise" (Isaiah 43:21). The Scriptures are filled with prayers giving praise, honor, glory and worship to God. As we pray with God's Word, we can the more easily become a people of praise.

**First Day—Psalm 150**
"Let everything that has breath praise the Lord."

**Second Day—Revelation 7:9-17**
"Praise and glory . . . to our God forever."

**Third Day—Daniel 3:52-90**
"And blessed is your holy and glorious name."

**Fourth Day—Ephesians 1:3-6**
". . . that all might praise the glorious favor he has bestowed on us in his beloved."

**Fifth Day—Hebrews 13:12-21**
"Through him let us continually offer God a sacrifice of praise."

**Sixth Day—Psalm 111**
"His praise endures forever."

**Seventh Day—Philippians 2:9-11**
"Every knee must bend . . . and every tongue proclaim to the glory of God the Father: Jesus Christ is Lord!"

## Thanksgiving

We cannot have a true celebration without a memorial. As we recall some important event, person or place, only then can we celebrate a memorial.

Thanksgiving Day is a memorial of God's loving, providential care. It brings to mind God's infinite bounty to us from the days of the pilgrims down to our very own.

Likewise, Scripture is not only a record of God's infinite bounty, but also a summons for us to render thanks to God.

One of our human failings is to take so very much for granted. How seldom we say, "Thank You," even though our hearts are grateful. Yet we know from experience how deeply ingratitude can wound.

How generous is God in bestowing his gifts upon us—life, breath, health, family and friends. How plenteous and rich are our harvests—not only for sustenance, but for our enjoyment as well.

We need to pause to recount God's loving, providential care. As we pray his Word, we are reminded of his bounteous gifts to us.

The Scriptures also remind us that God wants his children to thank him. On numerous occasions Jesus taught us by his examples as he turned to his Father in thanksgiving.

What greater gift is there than his Son and the divine life which he shares with us! How tremendous the gift of his Spirit dwelling within us! How gracious his love!

# Prayer of Thanskgiving

Jesus taught us the importance of rendering thanks to the Father. He offered thanks before some of his miracles— before the multiplication of the loaves, before raising Lazarus and before instituting the Holy Eucharist. He encouraged us to thank God constantly. We know from personal experience how painful ingratitude can be. Our Christian vocation calls us to be a grateful people.

**First Day—Psalm 30**
"O Lord, my God, forever will I give you thanks."

**Second Day—Luke 17:11-19**
The ingratitude of nine lepers: "Was there no one to return and give thanks to God except this foreigner?"

**Third Day—Colossians 3:12-17**
"Dedicate yourselves to thankfulness."

**Fourth Day—Sirach 51:1-12**
"I give you thanks, O God of my father."

**Fifth Day—1 Timothy 1:12-17**
"I thank Christ Jesus our Lord . . . that he has made me his servant."

**Sixth Day—1 Chronicles 29:10-13**
"Therefore, our God we give you thanks."

**Seventh Day—Psalm 138:1-5**
"I will give thanks to you, O Lord, with all my heart."

# WEEK 49

## God in Our World

One of the fruits of prayer is experiencing God as an integral part of our daily living. The fact that God himself is present objectively in our world and that he is working in it, makes it possible for us to experience his presence in our lives.

During these weeks of praying with Scripture, we have discovered God's will for how we are to live. We have chosen God by orienting our world toward him. And more important, God has chosen us by designing the world for us to live and work in.

In the first stage of praying with God's Word we heard God telling us how much he loves us. He loves us with a creative, providential love. He loves us with a forgiving, healing, redeeming love—regardless of what we have done. When we begin to realize God's gratuitous love for us, our response becomes more generous and more personal.

In the second phase we reflected on how God responded to man's needs. God prepared the world and his people for the gift of his Son. The incarnation is an on-going gift to the world. Jesus remains present among us and within us.

Thirdly, we contemplated the overwhelming truth that "God so loved the world that he gave his only Son" (John 3:16) and the Son so loved us that he gave his life for our redemption. "There is no greater love than this: to lay down one's live for one's friends" (John 15:13).

Lastly, we reflected on God's benevolence. In giving us his Spirit he provides for our every spiritual need, and in his Fatherly love he also supplies all of our temporal needs. "How much more will your heavenly Father give good things to anyone who asks him!" (Matthew 7:11).

# Intercessory Prayer

Jesus taught us to pray not only by word, but also by his example. He frequently went off to pray by himself. He prayed before all the important events of his public life. He encourages us to pray always; to step out in faith and ask for what is necessary for our salvation. We learn to pray only by praying. With the disciples let us also ask: "Lord, teach us to pray" (Luke 11:1).

**First Day—Matthew 7:7-11**
"Ask, and you will receive."

**Second Day—Matthew 18:19-20**
"If two of you join your voices on earth to pray for anything whatever, it shall be granted you."

**Third Day—Luke 22:39-46**
"In his anguish he prayed with all the greater intensity."

**Fourth Day—James 5:15-18**
"The fervent petition of a holy man is powerful indeed."

**Fifth Day—Philippians 4:4-7**
"Present your needs to God in every form of prayer."

**Sixth Day—Matthew 21:18-22**
"You will receive all that you pray for, provided you have faith."

**Seventh Day—Ephesians 6:18-20**
"Pray constantly and attentively for all in the holy company."

## Victory Over Death

Prayer is a relationship with God. As we spend more time in prayer, this relationship grows and becomes more intimate. As this relationship deepens it has a tremendous transforming power.

Praying with Scripture draws us into a personal relationship with our loving, gracious Father. He reveals himself as a kind, loving God who provides for us at every moment of our existence. He is a compassionate God who wants to forgive us more than we could even want to be forgiven.

His guiding hand leads us along our pilgrimage back to him — our Father. He gave his son who is "the way, and the truth, and the life" (John 14:6). He did not leave us orphans, but gave us his Holy Spirit to abide with us to mature, guide, strengthen and sanctify us.

As our relationship grows deeper in prayer, even death takes on a whole new dimension. Death is not to be feared but it is rather the doorway into our Father's arms.

Because of his deep relationship with God through prayer, Paul could cry out: "O death, where is your victory? O death, where is your sting?" (1 Corinthians 15:55).

In speaking of our victory over death, St. Paul says: "Thanks be to God who has given us the victory through our Lord Jesus Christ" (1 Corinthians 15:57).

# Commission—Spread The Good News

At the beginning of his public life Jesus invited his followers to *Come*. Come to him to be taught, to be formed, to acquire a whole new spiritual way of thinking, to put on the new man. After the Resurrection he commissioned them to *Go* and bring the Good News to all men. His invitation to us is the same: *Come* to him in prayer, and then *Go* to all men bringing the glad tidings of great joy.

**First Day—Matthew 28:19-20**
"Go, therefore and make disciples of all the nations. . . . And know that I am with you always, until the end of the world."

**Second Day—Luke 10:1-20**
"He who hears you, hears me."

**Third Day—Acts 10:34-43**
"He commissioned us to preach . . . and to bear witness."

**Fourth Day—Luke 24:46-49**
"Penance for the remission of sins is to be preached to all the nations."

**Fifth Day—Romans 10:13-21**
"How beautiful are the feet of those who announce the good news."

**Sixth Day—Ephesians 6:10-17**
"Stand fast, with . . . zeal to propagate the Gospel of peace."

**Seventh Day—2 Corinthians 4:1-7**
"We proclaim the truth openly."

# WEEK 51

## Render Constant Thanks

The letters in the New Testament give us an insight into the attitude which every Christian must have. St. Paul diligently guides us in forming a proper Christian mentality. Repeatedly he tells us we must be grateful. He says, "Name something you have that you have not received" (1 Corinthians 4:7). Obviously, we have nothing which we have not received; therefore, one of our duties is to be grateful to God for all his benevolence.

St. Paul encourages us to "pray in a spirit of thanksgiving" (Colossians 4:2), and to "render constant thanks" (1 Thessalonians 5:18). He tells us that every Christian should have a heart "overflowing with gratitude" (Colossians 2:7).

Faith is a gift from God. He has bestowed that gift upon us. In our baptism he invited us to become members of his family. He adopted us as his sons and daughters. This gives us our true dignity as persons and Christians. Since faith is a gift from God, St. Paul tells us we should always be "giving thanks to the Father for having made you worthy to share the lot of the saints in light" (Colossians 1:12).

St. Paul epitomizes much of this attitude when he says "Thanks be to God for his indescribable gift!" (2 Corinthians 9:15).

# Seeing God in all Things

God is present to us in many different ways. He is dwelling within us. He surrounds us with the beauty of his creation. His providential love accompanies us at every moment of the day. His power and presence become very apparent to us on many occasions. He is a transcendent God, but is also immanent in our lives. A frequent pause throughout the day will help us focus our attention on his abiding presence with us and within us.

**First Day—Sirach 17:1-27**
"His majestic glory their eyes beheld."

**Second Day—Psalm 8**
"How glorious is your name over all the earth."

**Third Day—Romans 11:33-36**
"How deep are the riches and the wisdom and the knowledge of God!"

**Fourth Day—Psalm 148**
"His majesty is above earth and heaven."

**Fifth Day—James 1:16-19**
"Every genuine benefit comes from above."

**Sixth Day—Psalm 104**
"O Lord, my God, you are great indeed!"

**Seventh Day—Romans 1:19-23**
"God's eternal power and divinity have become visible."

# Paul Thanks God

St. Paul taught us in many different ways how to live a Christian life. He taught us that we must be grateful to God at all times.

In the introduction to nearly all his letters he expressed thanks. This expression serves as an admonition to us to do the same.

Paul was grateful to God for the gift of faith given to the Romans: "First of all, I give thanks to God through Jesus Christ for all of you because your faith is heralded throughout the world" (Romans 1:8).

The Corinthians were especially dear to Paul. He was thankful for God's gift to them: "I continually thank my God for you because of the favor he has bestowed on you in Christ Jesus" (1 Corinthians 1:4).

The same note of gratitude permeates Paul's letter to the Philippians: "I give thanks to my God every time I think of you which is constantly, in every prayer I utter" (Philippians 1:3-4).

St. Paul was grateful to God for all his co-workers. Many times he thanked God for every one of them. He reminds Timothy of his gratitude to God for "Timothy, my child whom I love. . . . I thank God, the God of my forefathers whom I worship with a clear conscience, whenever I remember you in my prayers—as indeed I do constantly night and day" (2 Timothy 1:2-3).

Paul also tells us that "all Scripture is . . . useful for teaching . . . and training in holiness" (2 Timothy 3:16). Thus we learn gratitude from the example and attitude of the great apostle of the Gentiles.

# Future Bliss

Death is the doorway into life of perfect union with God. Love wants to be united with the person loved. As we enter this divine union, God shares with us to the full his divine life and love. Jesus said: "I came that they might have life and have it to the full" (John 10:10). In this life we share only partially in the life of God, but to an infinite degree in heaven.

**First Day—Revelation 14:13**
"Happy now are the dead who die in the Lord!"

**Second Day—John 11:25-26**
"I am the resurrection and the life."

**Third Day—1 Corinthians 15:53-55**
"Death is swallowed up in victory."

**Fourth Day—Wisdom 3:1-8**
"The souls of the just are in the hand of God."

**Fifth Day—1 Thessalonians 4:13-17**
"Thenceforth we shall be with the Lord unceasingly."

**Sixth Day—John 12:24-26**
"Unless the grain of wheat falls to the earth and dies, it remains just a grain of wheat."

**Seventh Day—Romans 6:1-11**
". . . so that, just as Christ was raised from the dead by the glory of the Father, we too might live a new life."